CULTIVATING
SELF-DEVELOPMENT

David Megginson and Vivien Whitaker

David Megginson is a research fellow at Sheffield Business School. He is the author of *Self-Development* (with Mike Pedler), *A Manager's Guide to Coaching* (with Tom Boydell), *Mentoring in Action* (with David Clutterbuck), and *The Line Manager as Developer* (with Malcolm Leary). He is co-author of reports on *Developing the Developers* and *Learning Processes in the Chartered Surveying Profession*. He is an elected member of AMED's Council, chair of the European Mentoring Centre, and a member of the Advisory Board of Mentoring Directors Ltd. He has also been an assessor of the National Training Awards.

Vivien Whitaker works with people in organisations to assist them in improving their effectiveness. She lectures, researches, and consults at Sheffield Hallam University. Her focus is on developing more effective ways of managing and working. In a recent book – *Managing People* – she created new frameworks for customer-focused management, with the manager providing a service to staff, who provide in turn a service to customers. Her current research is on ways of maximising personal effectiveness in the virtual office.

Vivien and David have together developed, managed, and facilitated many self-development programmes.

In the TRAINING ESSENTIALS series leading experts focus on the key issues in contemporary training. The books are thoroughly comprehensive, setting out the theoretical background while also providing practical guidance to meet the 'hands-on' needs of training practitioners. They are essential reading for trainers and for students working towards training qualifications – N/SVQs, and Diploma and Certificate courses in Training and Development.

Other titles in the series include:

Creating a Training and Development Strategy Andrew Mayo

Delivering Training Suzy Siddons

Designing Training Alison Hardingham

Developing Learning Materials Jacqui Gough

Evaluating Training Peter Bramley

Facilitation Skills Frances and Roland Bee

Designing Training Alison Hardingham

Introduction to Training Penny Hackett

The Institute of Personnel and Development is the leading publisher of books and reports for personnel and training professionals, students, and all those concerned with the effective management and development of people at work. For full details of all our titles please telephone the Publishing Department:

tel. 0181-263 3387
fax 0181-263 3850
e-mail publish@ipd.co.uk

The catalogue of all IPD titles can be viewed on the IPD website:
http://www.ipd.co.uk

TRAINING ESSENTIALS

CULTIVATING
SELF-DEVELOPMENT

David Megginson and
Vivien Whitaker

INSTITUTE OF PERSONNEL AND DEVELOPMENT

Design and typesetting by Paperweight
Printed in Great Britain by
The Cromwell Press, Wiltshire

British Library Cataloguing in Publication Data
A catalogue record for this book is available from the
British Library

ISBN
0-85292-640-5

INSTITUTE OF PERSONNEL
AND DEVELOPMENT

IPD House, Camp Road, London SW19 4UX
Tel.: 0181 971 9000   Fax: 0181 263 3333
Registered office as above. Registered Charity No. 1038333.
A company limited by guarantee. Registered in England No. 2931892.

Contents

Dedication

This book is dedicated to all the people who have worked with us on self-development programmes. We thank them for their courage, their risk-taking, and the changes they have made in their lives. We are all on a journey of continuing self-development. We are enjoying living life adventurously – we hope you are, too.

Acknowledgements

We would like to thank the following people who have supported the thinking that has gone into this book: Kath Attenborough, Nicolina Bartels-King, Colin Beard, Anne Brackley, Tom Boydell, Tim Casserley of Texaco, Anne Cordwent of the IPD, Peter Collett, Neil Donovan, Michael Dower, Ian Flemming, Roger Harrison, Melanie Hollinshead, Stella Jackson of the London Borough of Lewisham, Bianca Kübler and Phil Dickinson of ICL, Nicky Keogh and the staff of Keyo Agricultural Services, Suzanne Leckie, Philip Lewer, Fides Matzdorf, Stephen McCarroll, Ruth Marchington, Jenny Joy-Matthews, Gareth Morgan, Janice Nunn, Mike Pedler, Mike Pupius, Mark Ramsbottom and the staff of LSU, Phil Samuels, John Stannard, and Gladys Whitaker. Special thanks go to Joan Butt for our illustrations. We are also especially grateful to Katherine and Edward Megginson for the tolerance they have shown to a pair of distracted authors and for their burgeoning capacity to develop and look after themselves.

1

What is Self-Development?

Self-development is an approach that emphasises the importance of lifelong learning. It recognises that we all have a great potential for learning and for changing what we do.

It differs from traditional, instructor-centred approaches by giving the primary responsibility for learning to learners themselves: they are shown how to use a variety of methods to diagnose their needs and then create an action plan for implementing change. Such an approach has become popular and successful because it helps people to adapt to, and enjoy, the new challenges of organisational life.

Continuous learning

> Organisations that do not learn faster than the rate of change in the environment will eventually die.
>
> Reg Revans[1]

The environment in which we work is changing more rapidly than ever before. If we are to capitalise on these changes, we need to become very skilled at learning in order to be able to respond quickly and appropriately. So that they might rise to this challenge learners are encouraged to use the experiential learning cycle[2] (see Figure 1) to assist their learning from experience and their planning for the future. Self-development focuses on this

Figure 1

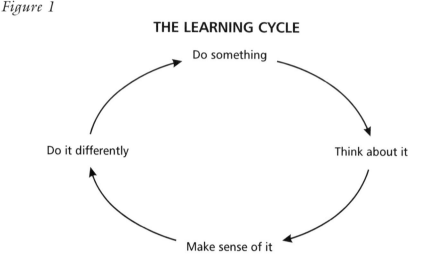

THE LEARNING CYCLE

cyclical process of learning, which encourages us to build the ability to take responsibility and be proactive – initiating action, rather than being reactive – in the way we work.

Being proactive assists us in gaining more awareness of our power to respond to any situation by recognising our own role in influencing its outcome. Self-development challenges us to recognise, and to own, our responsibility in influencing outcomes by taking risks and doing things differently. Such risk-taking can begin in small ways. One learner beginning a self-development programme started doing things differently when he was driving to work on his usual route and found that there were roadworks and delays. Normally he would have sat in the queue waiting, but he decided to take a risk and turn into sideroads that he did not know and find his way to work intuitively. This was so successful that he felt confident in doing other things differently too.

Our approach to change

> Everything flows and everything is constantly changing. You cannot step twice in the same river, for other waters are constantly flowing on.
>
> Heraclitus, 500 BC

The rate of change has increased since the time of Heraclitus but the philosophy has remained the same: everything and everyone is constantly changing.[3] Self-development helps us to recognise that change is a natural and inevitable part of our working lives, stimulating us to be aware of our own role in responding to it. It also assists us to take a holistic view of change and to focus on our organisation's need for change and development.

Charles Handy illustrates the need for organisational change by using the Sigmoid curve (see Figure 2).[4] He suggests that this s-shaped curve can be applied to all organisations. It describes how organisations start growing falteringly, grow more vigorously, and then wane – unless their members plan significant change.

Figure 2

THE SIGMOID CURVE OF ORGANISATIONAL LIFE

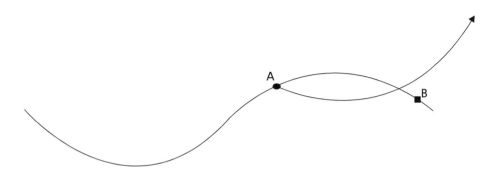

Handy argues that planning change often starts at the wrong time: when organisations are beginning to wane and to become less effective (point B in Figure 2). He advocates changing while they are still on the up (point A) so that they have the energy and resources to begin a new Sigmoid curve. Let us consider a concrete example of Handy's argument.

The Liverpool Students' Union (LSU) is a very proactive organisation that recognises the value of changing at point A, and is indeed continually seeking opportunities for change. The Union did some research on its past income patterns and became aware that every time it launched a new service or product (about every three years), they began a new Sigmoid curve, and their income mirrored the beginning of the curve. Their growth could therefore be seen as a series of Sigmoid curves (see Figure 3).

Figure 3

GROWTH OF LIVERPOOL STUDENTS' UNION

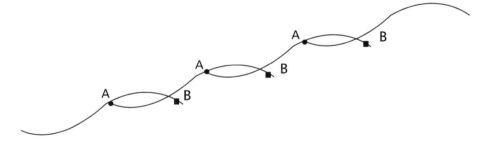

What this demonstrates is that continuous learning and development are core elements of LSU's culture; staff gain customer feedback and are constantly seeking ways to change and improve their services to create greater customer satisfaction. Self-development can, therefore, help to create flexible and responsive staff who feel empowered to create appropriate change.

New ways of working

> The information revolution will be as significant in its impact on the way we work as the industrial revolution was at the end of the last century.
>
> Tom Peters[5]

The way we work is changing dramatically. Information technology has helped organisations to operate more effectively in global markets by using virtual management. It has automated many of our processes and transformed methods of product design. Many people throughout the Western economies are also changing their work location and their style of work. In the USA, for example, 18 per cent of companies now operate working-from-home programmes, while half of the workforce in the European Union has limited term or part-time contracts, or is self-employed.

A recent survey of home-working at ICL has shown that staff find this an effective and enjoyable way of working. The biggest growth in such telework has however been in 'satellite' offices either on out-of-town industrial estates or, in some cases, in another country where back-office information-processing or telephone sales work is located away from corporate headquarters.

Our terms and conditions of employment are also changing. Many organisations are restructuring to make themselves 'flatter' or smaller, semi-autonomous work units. Multiskilled, self-directed teams are being developed because they are more flexible and responsive than those found in more traditional styles of production management. More work is being outsourced to other organisations, and agency and short-term contract work is increasing.

The result of all these changes is that jobs for life and unquestioned job security are now things of the past. Yet all is not gloom. During the process of self-development learners create a portfolio of their skills and knowledge.

This helps them to appreciate that security rests no longer with a particular job but in their own ability constantly to develop skills and knowledge so that their portfolio continues to match the requirements of the market-place.

Many professional associations, such as the IPD, encourage their members to develop portfolios, which give details of their qualifications, experience, and continuing professional development. Professions such as nursing and engineering require their members to maintain 'continuing development portfolios' throughout their careers.

Some organisations recognise that they can no longer guarantee long-term employment in such uncertain times as the present, and so they offer a new commitment to employees: to enhance employability through supporting self-development programmes. This provides a way for staff to develop both their competence and confidence, and frequently stimulates career development. (Those who cannot gain support for their self-development within their organisation or through their professional association may choose to create a self-development group with friends or colleagues.)

Growing in a holistic way

Self-development is a holistic approach, because it involves our whole selves. Mike Pedler and Tom Boydell remind us that this approach involves both our outer selves (which relate to other people) and our inner selves (which look at our own motivation, values and beliefs).[6] (See Figure 4.) They emphasise that we need to flow back and forth between our outer and inner selves if we are to learn and develop in a balanced way. We have used this model and integrated it with David Megginson and Mike Pedler's 'Steps to Development' to explain the initial dialogue between the inner and outer selves.[7]

Figure 4

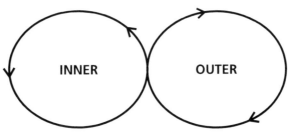

THE INTERACTION BETWEEN OUR INNER AND OUTER SELVES

Step 1

This starts with your inner self and focuses on your desire to learn. Be clear about what you want to learn: you may want to understand a new way of working, master a particular computer package, find better ways of working with your colleagues, or advance your career. Whatever you desire will be unique to you. You may have a whole list of things that you want to do differently; if so, think about putting them in some sort of order. Do not worry if this desire to change seems unfocused at first. The most important ingredient is a desire to do things differently. Until you have that, self-development cannot start.

Step 2

Think about why you are dissatisfied and what you want to do about it. Initial workshops on self-development programmes provide you with a number of ways to undertake self-diagnosis and clarify what you want to do. These may involve you in assessing your patterns of learning in addition to focusing on what you want to learn, so that you can clarify your learning preferences and learning blockages.

Typically we have four choices when we are dissatisfied:

1   Put up with things.
2   Leave.

3   Get others to change.

4   Change ourselves.

Self-development programmes are designed for people who give a lot of attention to option 4.

Step 3

Choose your appropriate method of development and set some realistic goals that describe how you would like to be different. Write them down in a measurable form so that you can assess your progress.

Step 3 and a half

Move from your inner to your outer self and take a risk, related to the goals you have set. This may mean asking someone to give you feedback on your performance at work, or doing something you have never done before. The risk should challenge you to go beyond your experience to try something new and learn from it.

This is a symbolic step that helps you prove to yourself that you are able to change. This is your first task, and it does not have to be a big risk; the intention is to get a feel of what it is like to initiate your own development. Once you have taken a small risk, it feels easier to commit yourself to making other changes in the future.

Step 4

Design your learning process based on your goals, and find the appropriate resources and support to enable you to achieve those goals. If you are on a self-development programme paid for by your employer, some of these issues may already have been resolved for you.

Step 5

Share your goals with others and recruit people to help you: colleagues, friends, people with particular skills and resources, members of a professional association, and partners and family. Other participants on your self-development programme may be particularly useful in providing mutual support and challenge.

Step 6

Persevere with your learning programme. It can sometimes be really hard to stick to it, with work (and perhaps family) pressures making their demands on your time.

Sometimes it is important to focus on your inner self at this stage and to recall why you think these changes are important for your long-term development. This may help you to put short-term pressures, which might interrupt your development, into perspective.

Step 7

Assess yourself against your goals. What have you learnt from your successes and failures? What has happened that you did not expect, and how has that affected you?

Return to your outer self and gain feedback from others – assessing progress is a healthy process. You need this information to decide whether you are on track or whether you need to revise your goals.

Celebrate success with those who have helped you, and then return to Step 1 to begin your next development plan.

Self-development is a lifelong process. It does not finish when a formal course ends. It is a way of planning and working that becomes so challenging and exciting that you want to integrate it into your life on a continuous basis.

In brief

In this chapter we have introduced the concept of self-development:

> Self-development is an approach that emphasises the importance of lifelong learning. It recognises that we all have a great potential for learning and for changing what we do.

We have explored four ways in which self-development helps people to adapt to and enjoy the new challenges of organisational life. It:

- encourages continuous learning
- makes us reconsider our attitude to change
- helps us to adapt to new ways of working
- enables us to grow in a holistic way.

References

1   GARRATT B. *The Learning Organization*. London, Fontana. (1987)

2   WHITAKER V. *Managing People*. London, Harper Collins. (1994)

3   *Ibid.*

4   HANDY C. *The Empty Raincoat*. London, Hutchinson. (1994)

5   Quoted from 'In search of excellence', *The Money Programme*, BBC2. (28 October 1995)

6   PEDLER M. and BOYDELL T. *Managing Yourself*. Aldershot, Gower. (1990)

7   MEGGINSON D. and PEDLER M. *Self-Development – A facilitator's guide*. Maidenhead, McGraw-Hill. (1992)

Conditions for Success

Self-development is at the core of successful professional development. In this chapter we describe what makes for successful self-development programmes, so that you can examine your organisation or personal situation and decide whether self-development is appropriate to your circumstances.

The principal stakeholders of a self-development programme are the

- participants
- organisation
- facilitators of the programme.

We shall look at the conditions for success for each of these stakeholders.

Participants: conditions for success
Condition 1: encourage self-development beliefs

During our work with Texaco we were challenged to identify the characteristics of individuals who were successful self-developers. We recognised that successful self-developers shared a set of developmental beliefs. They could say of themselves:

- I can make a difference at work.
- I can develop myself to do and be more than I am at present.

■ I am aware of the impact of my own actions and can gather information about this from the feedback of others.

If participants hold these beliefs strongly then it will be hard to *stop* their self-development. If they do not share these beliefs then it will be important to examine what beliefs they do hold about development and awareness, and then offer them alternative models of self-development to experiment with.

Condition 2: be open to new understanding

Self-development helps us to look at and to change both the way we think and the way we do things. Many initial workshops on self-development programmes use a variety of methods to help participants to open their minds to new possibilities and to develop skills in 'reframing' – looking at issues in new ways. This works better if participants come to the programme *wanting* to make changes.

Not everyone does want to. We have encountered managers who have come to programmes thinking they will be a comfortable break from work, or that their role is merely to set an example for others in need of training. Typical of this attitude was a senior manager who attended a programme but carried on with his office work (on his knee) rather than listen to the speaker.

It is a focused and open mind that learns most effectively.

Condition 3: be prepared to take action

Gareth Morgan stresses that action is as important as understanding.[1] He argues that to experience change means to combine both new understanding and new action, but that when we plan change, although we often give a lot of thought to creating new understanding, we give less to action.

Morgan encourages us to think about our recent

experiences of change and to analyse their components. We have found that those who are focused on both new understanding *and* new action are the most successful in meeting the demands of change.

The recognition of the importance of new action leads us to design most of our self-development programmes using the principles of 'action learning'. Scott Inglis describes this as:

> ...a process which develops people and organisations, using important issues confronting the organisation as a vehicle for doing so.[2]

Participants develop themselves by working on live issues confronting them or their part of an organisation. This is a social process, participants analysing problems and learning from each other and a facilitator in a small group known as an 'action learning set'. Sets typically meet once a month for half a day over a period of six to nine months.

The learning achieved during these sets is explained using the following formula (Revans expanded by Inglis):

$$L = P + Q + I$$

where

L = learning
P = programmed knowledge
Q = the ability to pose 'insightful' questions
I = implementation.

Learning is achieved by:

- sharing appropriate knowledge
- high-quality probing
- debate
- experimenting with new things in the workplace
- monitoring success and reporting back to the set.

These principles are explained in more detail in Chapter 5.

Condition 4: focus on using your 15 per cent

W. Edwards Demming studied the question of quality in organisations for many years and analysed the amount of influence that any person, in any job, had over his or her part of the organisation. His results indicated that 85 per cent of a person's influence was constrained by structure, systems, and procedures, leaving just *15 per cent available to promote change*.

Demming's statistical research concluded that, surprisingly, these percentages apply just as much to a managing director as to a newly appointed school-leaver, the difference being of course that the actual size of the responsibility of a newly appointed school-leaver is much smaller.

Gareth Morgan has developed the idea of 15 per cent influence as a metaphor for 'high-leverage' change. He encourages us to look for those opportunities where we can influence change and create a significant difference in our part of an organisation. Fifteen per cent opportunities do not necessarily involve a lot of work: they come from thinking strategically and recognising when the time is right, or who the right person is to influence. For example, if you are one of the first contributors to an e-mail discussion on a subject, you have a greater chance to shape the debate; and if you circulate important material for discussion well in advance of a meeting rather than during it, you are more likely to influence your colleagues. The person who sets the framework for the debate has a disproportionate influence on the whole discussion.

We recommend that people actively search for 15 per cent opportunities as part of their planning at the beginning of each week, and then at the end of the week assess how influential they have been.

Philip Lewer, assistant director at Bradford Social Services, is someone who is very effective at using his 15 per cent influence. When he took over responsibility for community mental health services he was asked to make improvements – but without an increase in budget. He therefore sought ways of doing things differently by looking at all the existing systems and processes to see if these could be improved. He worked with his staff and transformed the service of applying to a mental health hostel. This process typically took six weeks and involved a social worker visiting relatives and preparing a report to be submitted to a committee, which would then make recommendations to the hostel manager. Lewer was able to identify that it was the hostel manager who made the crucial decision, and that if hospital records could be made available to the hostel manager he or she they would have sufficient information on which to base a decision. Through negotiation and network links with the appropriate NHS Trust, information could be downloaded electronically, and a decision that had previously taken six weeks and involved several people could be made within 10 minutes.

This is an important example for self-developers. When we are looking at ways of developing ourselves and doing things differently we need to focus on areas where we can use our 15 per cent influence to its fullest effect.

At this point try Table 1 on page 16 to assess your own (or others') readiness for self-development. The questionnaire is not intended to be a high-powered psychometric test to tell you what you are like. Rather, we encourage you to use it as a jumping-off point for self-exploration. When you have filled it out, you can ask yourself which issues you are happy with and which you would like to change.

Add up your score from Table 1: the higher your score, the readier you are likely to be for self-development. If you have reservations about our reasons for this on any of the questions, then this is probably a good sign in terms of self-development – having questions about the views of so-called experts! Have another look at the previous section, because as our rationale for each of the points is in there, in the same order as the questions.

Table 1

ARE YOU READY FOR SELF-DEVELOPMENT?

How ready we are to undertake personal self-development is influenced by our beliefs, the information we have, and our willingness to take action. These are all explored in this short questionnaire.

Ring the number which most closely describes your view of each item.

1 I believe I can make a difference at work	+2 +1 0 −1 −2	What I do makes no difference at work
2 I have ample scope for further personal development	+2 +1 0 −1 −2	I have developed all I am likely to
3 I have relatively little feedback from others about my work	+2 +1 0 −1 −2	I have a great deal of feedback from others about my work
4 I strongly want to make a lot of changes at work	+2 +1 0 −1 −2	Circumstances mean I do not see much chance of making changes at work
5 By opening myself up to colleagues' ideas I can begin to make a difference	+2 +1 0 −1 −2	There is not much scope for me to learn from colleagues about my work
6 I like doing new things, approaching problems in new ways	+2 +1 0 −1 −2	I like to explore ideas and frameworks
7 I shall learn more by asking better questions	+2 +1 0 −1 −2	I learn best by getting the solutions of experts
8 I help decide which issues are addressed in striving for improvement	+2 +1 0 −1 −2	Others always determine which issues are addressed in our improvement efforts

Organisations: conditions for success

Self-development programmes can be successful in organisations when one or more of a number of conditions applies:

Condition 1: when the culture encourages individual action

The managing director of one division of a company that had offered self-development to all its managers reported to us as follows on the effects of the programme:

> I want a culture that is completely open, where people can discuss, challenge the structure, where anything can be communicated, where people feel empowered, not at all afraid to do what is best for their customers. I do not see the self-development programme as separate from the corporate vision or our business objectives. It is one process of change and building a different culture. The programme is culturally consistent.

It is not surprising that in this division there was a very high and enthusiastic take-up of the programme.

Condition 2: when there is a commitment from management and staff to change the style of working

Bob Solberg, chairman of Texaco Ltd, has said:

> We have no choice but to accelerate our business so we take less time to realise the returns on the substantial investments we seek from the corporation. Recent changes have helped us to grow in confidence. Added success will embolden us further to take on the challenges of creating value in ways unthinkable just a few years ago. It is exciting to contemplate just how far, together, we are going to take the part of the business that has been entrusted to us.

In those sections of Texaco where an elaborate committee-oriented hierarchy existed this kind of leadership has provided an impetus for change. Yet it is necessary not only for the 'champion' to support these values but also for people generally in the organisation to believe that support for them will continue for some time.

Condition 3: when you want to groom a group of people for promotion

ICL developed a programme for those of its high-potential managers who had the capacity to move to general manager jobs. As well as the personal development agenda characteristic of self-development groups, these managers also learned to use a range of strategic tools from Ashridge Management College. Sometimes in the development network groups their attention was focused on using the tools to develop a vision and strategy for their part of the business. At other times they returned to their personal development agenda. Phil Dickinson, the programme architect, and his colleagues were happy to let the focus shift from one issue to the other as participants wished, because both pivotal aspects of the programme contributed to the goal of preparing these highly energetic and talented individuals for the teamwork required in senior management positions.

Condition 4: when learners can take on special projects after the formal programme

One of the ways in which the Employment Service showed commitment to its head office development programme (HODP) was to have John Turner, deputy chief executive, involved from the start. He was there at the initial workshop and joined the group again during their half-day session with line managers (see Chapter 5 for details). During this session it was suggested that the group make a presentation to the senior management board to increase the powerholders' awareness of the programme.

Turner was so impressed with the drive and commitment of several members of the group that he involved them in special project work at the end of the formal programme. This gave participants a tremendous boost, because they had new projects in which to develop their newly acquired skills.

Condition 5: when a manager wants to create a different way of working within his or her sphere of control

Nicky Keogh, an owner-manager of a successful small company, was bored. So was his management team – things ran smoothly, profits were good, but there was little personal growth or challenge. So many able people left to go elsewhere.

Encouraged by his wife, Nicky commenced an MBA and learnt about self-development. He began to create ideas about how he wanted to change, and then recognised that if he got his whole team focused on self-development they could transform the way in which they did things.[3]

We worked with Nicky and his team, running three workshops over three months. The logistics were complicated, because they all needed to be involved but they could not simply shut down the office – so the workshops were run in the office while Nicky's wife fielded telephone calls.

The workshops focused on both self-development and creating a learning organisation where everyone had the opportunity to develop themselves while working towards developing the company. Roles were changed, lots of delegation took place, and plans for business diversification were developed. Nicky agreed to fund any training needed, and each member of staff became involved in some self-development activity. The atmosphere within the office changed and people began to enjoy coming to work.

This new approach was tested when the company's major customer withdrew their contract, deciding to take the work in-house. The team was able to speed up its plans for diversification, think creatively, and make appropriate changes quickly. With hindsight, Nicky felt that without the changes brought about by their self-development activities the company would probably have had to cease trading. The newly shaped company is now operating very successfully.

Condition 6: when self-development contrasts with the current culture

Michael Dower had been national park officer for the Peak National Park for five years when he chose to start a programme of change within the organisation. The purpose was to release the potential of the board's officers more fully than before. The staff of the Peak National Park were very talented, but he considered that they were constrained by the bureaucratic structures within the organisation.

A process of consultation and diagnosis was undertaken. The change proposed included action-learning-based management development programmes, which began with senior managers (including Dower) and which were then cascaded down the organisation.

Condition 7: when an autonomous group of individuals can do it for themselves

One of the trends of the 1990s has been the proliferation of professional organisations that have banded together to form alliances for learning. An early example was the social work managers' action learning programme in Nottinghamshire.[4] A more recent example is the collaborative inquiry group at Sheffield Hallam University made up of volunteers from departments as diverse as business, engineering, education, social science and cultural studies. They meet monthly to explore issues of learning design, research, and teaching, as well as more personal concerns about career and life purpose.

At a time when many of their colleagues are complaining of alienation, overwork and repressive managerialism those in the collaborative enquiry group open up possibilities for sharing, reflection, and action. One member of the group said in his long career at Sheffield this was the first time it felt as if he was in a university! The sharing of different perspectives and world views in a climate of support and mutual respect is a rare and valuable experience.

When not to adopt self-development within your organisation

Do not adopt this approach if:

▌ *the balance between fear and challenge within your organisation is overwhelmingly towards fear*. It is so much harder to make changes in a climate of fear than it is when confidence and a modicum of personal security are present. During a visit to Britain in 1995, Roger Harrison, the respected US consultant and writer on organisational development and self-directed learning, said that encouraging openness in many organisations at present is a recipe for a blood-bath. The appropriate response to this situation is to teach managers and others how to defend themselves from undue pressure and abuse.

▌ *some of the powerholders within your organisation are actively opposed to self-development*. In one organisation in which we have worked the programme, as well as having many individual benefits, also influenced climate, culture, and systems. At this point the chief executive left (using what he had learned from the change programme to do a bigger and better job elsewhere), but his successor was quite unwilling to sustain the momentum of organisational change. Although the programme continued to benefit individuals the corporate momentum was lost.

In these circumstances you are well advised to resolve these differences before you start, or to find a different, mutually agreeable, approach and set of objectives.

■ *People are going to be coerced into attending the programme.* The motivation for successful self-development programmes comes largely from within. If people are resisting attendance they may contribute little and so gain little in return. They may also have a demotivating effect on more committed participants who want to learn, change, and take risks. We came across people in one organisation who called themselves 'typical company *x* volunteers', by which they meant that, although the programme was billed as voluntary, refusal to attend would have been a career threatening decision.

■ *You have a very limited budget.* It is difficult to plan all the costs associated with self-development, because you cannot foresee every participant's needs. Costs involve not just running a start-up course and funding action-learning sets. They may also include supporting individuals when they are trying new things in their part of the organisation, eg assisting with teambuilding to resolve old resentments and problems or to introduce new styles of working.

Table 2 opposite is a tool for assessing your organisation's readiness for self-development. As with the individual self-development activity earlier in this chapter, (see Table 1, page 16) it gives you an indication of issues to consider in preparing your organisation for self-development, rather than offering a magic formula that will tell you whether to go for it or not.

Table 2

IS YOUR ORGANISATION READY FOR SELF-DEVELOPMENT?

1 Our organisation is open to new ideas	+2	+1	0	−1	−2	Our organisation strongly resists new ideas	
2 People are willing to act on their own initiative	+2	+1	0	−1	−2	Personal initiative is frowned upon	
3 New developments at work cause excitement	+2	+1	0	−1	−2	New developments at work are feared	
4 When we try something new, we follow it through	+2	+1	0	−1	−2	There are always flavours of the month being started and then dropped	
5 People who succeed here do so by growing the business and developing themselves	+2	+1	0	−1	−2	We train people only in order to improve the business	
6 Development initiatives are supported and seen through by top management	+2	+1	0	−1	−2	Top management give (at best) a token endorsement of development initiatives	
7 Management are committed to finding new ways of working	+2	+1	0	−1	−2	Management accept that the way most people work cannot be changed	
8 Top management have a vision of valuing staff and releasing their potential	+2	+1	0	−1	−2	Top management see staff as needing to be controlled	
9 People can set and pursue their own development agenda	+2	+1	0	−1	−2	People can only develop in ways specified by the organisation	
10 Our organisation runs on respect and valuing people	+2	+1	0	−1	−2	Our organisation runs on fear	
11 Vested interests are committed to developing people	+2	+1	0	−1	−2	Vested interests are actively opposed to developing people	
12 People can choose how to pursue their own development	+2	+1	0	−1	−2	People are obliged to attend development events relevant to their jobs	
13 There are sufficient resources available to develop people	+2	+1	0	−1	−2	We have negligible resources available to develop people	

Facilitators: conditions for success

Facilitators for self-development programmes are sometimes sought from within an organisation. Alternatively, a skilled and experienced facilitator is employed in a consultancy role. Often a combination of internal and external facilitators is highly productive of learning. In any case, finding the right facilitator(s) for your programme can be crucial to its success, and in order to do that you need to be aware that a facilitator for a self-development programme should possess certain qualities.

Condition 1: experience in the analysis and diagnosis of organisational issues

Analytical and diagnostic skills are important in the first phases of a self-development programme, because the facilitator needs to talk with people in the organisation concerned to ensure that the programme is an appropriate solution to the organisational issue being addressed. (These skills are also needed when helping to identify possible solutions to organisational issues during discussions in action learning sets.) Beware of trainers who to sell you the concept of self-development as a catch-all solution to your organisational ills, and immediately produce details of a programme they have just run for another organisation!

The facilitator needs, furthermore, to have a holistic view of organisational development so that he or she can encourage participants to broaden and develop their understanding of their own organisation.

Condition 2: listening skills

When engaged in discussion with either individuals or groups it is essential for a facilitator to use highly attuned listening skills in order to know when it is appropriate to intervene, when to allow silence to develop, and when to draw others into the conversation. The facilitator's role is not necessarily a high-profile one; he or she can often create more learning for others by simply listening a lot of the time and intervening strategically.

Condition 3: excellent communication skills

Facilitators need to be skilled at engaging their audience, presenting new concepts, and encouraging debate and discussion in small and large groups. They also need to possess the personal and professional confidence to work with the most senior powerholders in the organisation.

Condition 4: ability to work with other facilitators

Many self-development programmes have a number of action learning sets operating concurrently, so several facilitators are required to work together on the same programme. The way these facilitators work is a crucial part of the programme, because they are models for the concepts that they are introducing to their learners.

Condition 5: skill at dealing with conflict and emotional issues

When looking at the way in which we think about things we sometimes discover issues from our past that are unresolved, and that are therefore hindering our development. Such issues rarely emerge neatly: they are often hidden behind other issues. A skilled facilitator can help a participant by looking for the 'real problem' lying behind the 'presenting problem' and by giving support as he or she works on finding an appropriate solution.

Condition 6: to encourage a wide range of options

Facilitators are not advisers. It is not their role to solve problems. Their role is to develop discussion and direct debate in a way that encourages the fullest possible range of options around any issue. The point is that this allows participants to choose the most appropriate solution themselves.

Condition 7: active engagement in their own development

Being a facilitator on a self-development programme is a challenging role, because you are required to 'practise what you preach' and to model the kind of approach to professional development that you are recommending to participants. It is sometimes appropriate for facilitators to share some of their own professional experience of self-development.

Table 3 enables you to assess your readiness to become a facilitator of self-development.

Table 3

ARE YOU READY TO FACILITATE SELF-DEVELOPMENT?

1 I am able to identify and address organisational as well as individual issues	+2	+1	0	−1	−2	I am primarily able to identify and address individual issues
2 I see self-development as one of a range of development initiatives I can help with	+2	+1	0	−1	−2	I see self-development as the key route to developing people
3 I am happy to listen and allow others in a group to offer help	+2	+1	0	−1	−2	I feel a strong need to offer my insight and understandings to a group
4 I like to use silence in a group to think through what is happening	+2	+1	0	−1	−2	I am very uncomfortable with silence in a group
5 I am confident and clear in offering my views at all levels	+2	+1	0	−1	−2	I find offering my views at some levels difficult
6 I am good at spotting the hidden issues behind what people say	+2	+1	0	−1	−2	I often miss what people are getting at if they are not clear and open
7 I can usually identify the best solution when someone presents a problem	+2	+1	0	−1	−2	I am happy for people to explore a range of solutions to their problems
8 I am actively engaged in my own development	+2	+1	0	−1	−2	I am so busy helping others that I have little time for my own development

In brief

In this chapter we have outlined the conditions for successful self-development programmes so that you can undertake a comparative diagnosis of your organisation or situation and decide whether self-development is the most appropriate method of professional development for your circumstances.

We have described the conditions for success for the principal stakeholders of a self-development programme, namely the:

▮ participants
▮ organisation
▮ facilitators of the programme.

Tables 1 to 3 are questionnaires for each of these stakeholders in the self-development process, and are themselves a summary of the key issues in this chapter.

References

1   MORGAN G. *A Day with Gareth Morgan*. Seminar, Salford University. (January 1996)

2   INGLIS S. *Making the Most of Action Learning*. Aldershot, Gower. (1994)

3   MEGGINSON D., JOY-MATTHEWS J. and BANFIELD P. *Human Resource Development*. London, Kogan Page, pp 41–45. (1993)

4   COPE K., DAVIES S., GARTON M., HARRIS B., JARVIS A., PEARCE D. and SIMPSON A. *'Personal experience of a manager's self-development group'*, pp 70–94 in PEDLER M., BURGOYNE J. & and BOYDELL T. *Applying Self-development in Organisations*. Hemel Hempstead, Prentice-Hall. (1988)

3

Self-Development and Personal Change

**Warning: participating in a self-development
programme might change your life**

We hope it will. We have worked with many people who have chosen to make significant changes in the way they work, the way they interact with others, and the way they run their lives.

Initially some of these changes may not seem big in themselves. However, they have created dramatic improvements. For example, one very reserved manager, who previously went to his desk every morning without communicating with anybody, decided to say hello to each of his staff as he passed their desk each morning. This small change created such a positive response that the manager was encouraged to hold regular team meetings to discuss work allocation. As trust built up in these meetings, the team felt able to discuss long-standing unresolved issues that had inhibited team performance.

Another participant, who felt very alienated at work and was even planning to emigrate, chose to talk with his colleagues about new approaches to management. These ideas were so enthusiastically received that he was asked to talk to his boss's boss. This senior manager liked his suggestions so much that he decided that the whole department needed to adopt this approach. He asked the participant to take responsibility for implementing these changes.

There are many other similar stories that could be told. The important factor in each of them is that all the participants took a risk and did something differently. However, we are not suggesting that anyone takes unconsidered risks. Self-development is a way of identifying your areas of dissatisfaction and taking action about them in a planned way, with appropriate support.

The learner driver metaphor

Suzanne Leckie, an experienced self-developer, stresses the importance of preparing the ground for self-development.[1] She has created a framework for doing this based on the learner driver metaphor (see Figure 5).

Figure 5

THE LEARNER DRIVER METAPHOR

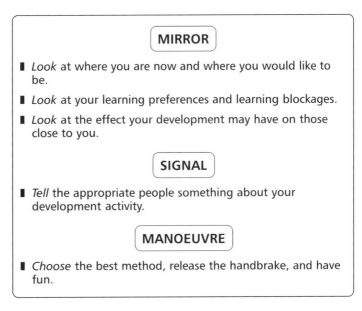

MIRROR

▌ *Look* at where you are now and where you would like to be.

▌ *Look* at your learning preferences and learning blockages.

▌ *Look* at the effect your development may have on those close to you.

SIGNAL

▌ *Tell* the appropriate people something about your development activity.

MANOEUVRE

▌ *Choose* the best method, release the handbrake, and have fun.

The easy-to-remember sequence of 'mirror, signal, manoeuvre' is helpful to us when we are at Step 1 of the seven-and-a-half steps to self-development (see Chapter 1, page 7).

MIRROR: *look at where you are now and where you would like to be*

When at Step 1 people are beginning to identify their areas of dissatisfaction. At this point we often ask participants to draw a picture of how they see themselves at work in a year's time. A period of one year is used because this seems a realistic time-span and often fits in with corporate planning.

Drawing uses the right, creative side of our brain and may often highlight something that we may not reveal through writing. The exercise is not about artistic skill – it is about thinking spatially and in images and metaphors. Stick people, line drawings, and speech bubbles are to be encouraged (see Figure 6, opposite)! Participants discuss their drawings in pairs and help one another to interpret what they have drawn. From this they begin to identify what they need to do differently in order to achieve their vision.

The manager who drew our example in Figure 6 saw himself as a magician and felt that this was a positive image: he was able to make things work when others could not, he was perceived as a bright and amusing character, and so on. His partner on a self-development workshop was able to help him to develop the metaphor of the magician in the context of his role as an internal IT consultant and draw out both the insights and limitations of this metaphor. Some of these insight included a need to:

∎ think about the way the 'magician's' internal customers perceived him
∎ check whether he was unwittingly using jargon when talking with his customers

Figure 6

A MANAGER'S DRAWING OF
'HOW I SEE MYSELF AT WORK IN ONE YEAR'S TIME'

- consider how accessible he was to his customers – did it seem as if he disappeared in a puff of smoke at just the wrong moment?
- demystify the use of IT when talking to customers so that they could more readily own and use the processes for themselves.

Another participant saw herself as the leader of a team of mountain climbers who were roped together, striving for the summit. By asking questions about this image, her partner was able to help her to develop this metaphor and realise that there was not just one mountain: this was the first mountain of a range of mountains or projects that her team would tackle together. The rope that held the party together proved a rich area to explore. What were the qualities that held them together? What did the project leader need to do to strengthen this rope in reality? Being roped together emphasised the mutual dependency: if one person fell they could pull everyone with them. In the event of someone falling, could the rope be fastened to an outcrop or would the leader bear the full weight of the team?

Once the drawings have been discussed we ask each participant to create a 'dissatisfaction mind-map' or spider diagram that highlights what needs to be changed in order for them to move to how they want to be at the end of the programme. This mind-map often reveals practical difficulties to be overcome, new skills that need to be practised, and networks of relationships to be developed (see Figure 7).

Figure 7

EXAMPLE OF A MANAGER'S DISSATISFACTION MIND-MAP

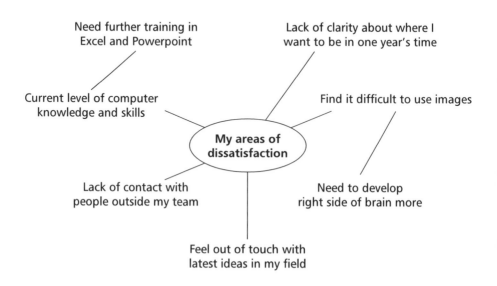

Need further training in Excel and Powerpoint

Lack of clarity about where I want to be in one year's time

Current level of computer knowledge and skills

Find it difficult to use images

My areas of dissatisfaction

Lack of contact with people outside my team

Need to develop right side of brain more

Feel out of touch with latest ideas in my field

When people are aware of what they want to change, the next questions to ask are:

∎ What will help me to change?
∎ What will hinder my efforts to change?

Suzanne Leckie emphasises the importance of this stage. She says that although it is easy to start a self-development project full of enthusiasm and commitment many projects fail because insufficient time has been spent in identifying and overcoming obstacles to success. She recommends analysing learning blockages and our learning preferences so that we can identify what might trip us up along the way and make plans to avoid this.

MIRROR: *look at your learning preferences and learning blockages*

There is a range of ideas and models that we can use to explore the way we learn. These may include looking at our patterns of learning, the assumptions we make about learning, and looking at our learning habits.

We tend to take the way we learn for granted. We do not think about it or question it: we simply do it. So it is helpful to start by mapping the significant learning throughout our lives to look at what we enjoyed and why we found it enjoyable. We should also look at what we did not enjoy and why we felt discouraged from learning.

These experiences can be drawn in the form of a 'learning lifeline' (see Figure 8 on page 34). Starting with your earliest memories, record your positive learning experiences above the central horizontal line and your negative learning experiences below this line.

It is often the negative learning experiences that hold us back and prevent us from taking risks. They generate phrases like 'It's too hard', 'I'll never', or 'I'm not going to put my head above the parapet', all of which paralyse our progress. We refer to these phrases and the memories they drag in their train as 'excess baggage' – something that trips us up and hinders our learning. Recent research has suggested links between our excess baggage, our bad experiences, and our habits.[2]

Figure 8

THE START OF A LEARNING LIFELINE

Positive learning experiences

Acting in a play	Passing exam	Learning to fence	Left home	Second job

Age (years) - - - - - 9 - - -10 - - 11- - 12 - - - - - - -14 - -15- - - - - 18- - - - - - - - - 21- - - ▶

Being told you won't pass the exam	Everyone sings and you mime	Nice girl but not academic like her sister

Negative learning experiences

Eric, a senior manager in a financial institution, was having bad experiences – difficulties in communicating with his boss. He began to look at his habits and recognised that he had a combative, rather than co-operative, style of working with people. This brought him short-term success but often created long-term pain and alienation. Through exploration and discussion he realised that he was carrying some excess baggage from his past. He had had a lonely childhood during which he often felt unsupported, and so grew up believing that the world was full of 'monsters' that he had to fight. This excess baggage led him to regard his boss as a 'monster' rather than a colleague, hence his win-lose combative style of communication rather than a win-win attitude to work. As Eric's awareness of his excess baggage grew he was able to 'reframe' his image of his boss and enter into a more mutually beneficial and successful relationship with him.

Recognising excess baggage and letting go of it can be both liberating and energising. It is usually a gradual process, because changing behaviour requires both risk-taking and practice. The process can be assisted by looking at the assumptions we make about learning.[3] For instance, the following positive assumption can be very helpful in changing the way we learn:

> Individuals can do anything they want to do – if it interests them. If they don't know how to do it they can learn.[4]

Many of us have grown up with parents or guardians who have not reinforced this positive assumption throughout our early years. However, we can choose to adopt it when we want to liberate the way in which we learn in the future. Others may have been brought up with an explicitly stated or merely implied list of things that they were told they could not do.

When Vivien (Whitaker) began focusing on her self-development she realised that what she had done in her life had been constrained by an implied list of what 'nice girls' should not do. For example, she had inferred that nice girls *do not*:

- climb trees
- argue back
- swing on ropes over a river
- help themselves first ('you must help others first')
- work in Cotton Waste (the family business)
- go to London alone
- stand out in the crowd.

Such constraints are often unspoken but exist as assumptions created through religion, societal belief, class or professional norms, and other influences on upbringing.

By raising these assumptions to the level of consciousness, we can become aware of the extent to which they still influence our lives in subtle ways. But we can also identify what we need to do differently in order to let go of these messages.

Vivien has been working through her old messages by challenging them at both intellectual and physical levels. She started (aged 26) by swinging on ropes over a river; learning to ride a bike (aged 35); rock climbing and abseiling (aged 40); and paragliding (aged 42). These actions have helped to bring long-held assumptions and limitations to the fore so that they can be physically and intellectually let go.

It is sometimes helpful to use imagery in this process of letting go. One person with whom we were working, metaphorically packed a rucksack full of his list of constraints, which he felt that he had been 'shouldering' for many years. He then went to a bridge over a river and dropped his imaginary rucksack full of constraints into the water and watched them be carried away by the current. This helped him to begin subconsciously and consciously to separate himself from those constraints. He repeats this process whenever he feels the burden returning.

The use of metaphor helped another person to become aware that he felt 'branded' because he had failed his eleven-plus examination 20 years before. This constrained him in his work, because he perceived others as more intelligent than him, creating a 'You're OK, I'm not OK' relationship with people. He was also frustrated because he felt a 'block' every time he had to do some writing (for example, a report). These perceptions had stopped him from undertaking a degree or any professional qualifications. We worked with the image of a brand on his arm, and discussed when and how he could focus on healing this metaphorical scar. We have recently heard that he has been accepted on a part-time professional Masters degree and cannot wait to get started on his first assignment!

We can intellectually and practically let go of an old habit or change an assumption within 30 days if we practise the new behaviour daily. There will be times when we struggle to change our patterns of behaviour, in which case it may be comforting to remember Straangard's model of change (see Figure 9).[5]

Figure 9

STRAANGARD'S MODEL OF CHANGE

Phase I	*Phase II*	*Phase III*	*Phase IV*
Unconscious Incompetence	Conscious Incompetence	Conscious Competence	Unconscious Competence

Straangard argues that we move through four distinct phases when we change our habits of these, the phases of conscious incompetence and conscious competence are those in which we feel uncomfortable and need help from others – help that is particularly important during the stage of conscious competence when we are practising new ways of doing things but are not yet comfortable with the new behaviours.

David (Megginson) had been engaged in some research on learning patterns that helped him be aware that he tended to be a reactive rather than a proactive learner: he was good at reacting to opportunities that came up but he did not go out to create opportunities for himself. He decided to experiment and include a goal-setting exercise at the end of his early morning exercise routine to see if this made a difference. He practised this every day for a month.[6] At the end of the month he was able to see that the goal-setting exercise had helped him to focus on what he wanted to achieve each day. This enabled him to gain more of what he wanted. In fact it was so successful that he started setting goals for himself on a yearly basis, in addition to his daily planning, and incorporated this planning cycle into the IPD's Continuous Development framework when it was first published.

The exploration of these issues led to the development of the concept of 'planned and emergent learning'.[7] David suggests that there are two different approaches to learning:

■ *planned learning* – learners take responsibility for the direction of their development

■ *emergent learning* – learners respond to and learn from their experiences.

We all have the potential for both planned and emergent learning, but we typically focus on one more than on the other.

David has also identified four types of learner (see Figure 10):

■ *sleepers*, who show little initiative or response to their experiences

■ *warriors*, who plan their experiences but tend not to learn from them

■ *adventurers*, who respond to and learn from opportunities that come their way but tend not to create opportunities for themselves

■ *sages*, who both plan and learn from their experiences.

We describe planned learners as warriors because they have focus, direction, clarity and persistence. We call emergent learners adventurers because they have curiosity, flexibility, and opportunism, and because they live 'in the now'. Sages have a lot of both qualities, whereas sleepers have yet to develop much of either. Think about where you would place yourself on the matrix in Figure 10, opposite.

We all have the potential to develop within both styles of learning. When David created this model he was primarily an emergent learner (an adventurer); Vivien, in contrast, was primarily a planned learner (a warrior). The model helped us to look at the way we worked together. Up

Figure 10

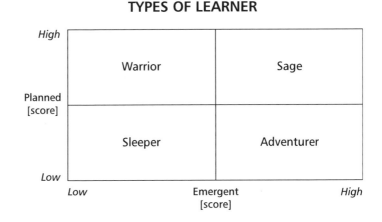

TYPES OF LEARNER

	Warrior	Sage
	Sleeper	Adventurer

Planned [score] — High / Low

Emergent [score] — Low / High

until then we had sometimes had fraught planning meetings on joint projects. Vivien would prepare by thinking through what she wanted out of a meeting; David would want to talk ideas through before he could crystallise his thoughts, and so would arrive with an open mind and an open agenda. On bad days Vivien used to insinuate that David was lazy; and he would accuse her of wanting to 'take over'. Happily the model shown in Figure 10 helped David to develop his planned learning (adventurer moving towards sage) and helped Vivien to increase her emergent learning (warrior moving towards sage). Our planning meetings are now more balanced and productive. (David has created a self-report questionnaire that assesses these learning dimensions and helps individuals to assess their current learning preferences and make plans to enhance their capacity as self-managed learners.[8])

MIRROR: *look at the effect your development may have on those close to you*

What we do can affect others. Each of us is like a stone thrown into a pond, the ripples we create touching others. If we begin to do things differently or begin to question accepted ways of doing things, this may affect our colleagues, staff, manager, friends, and family.

In some of the programmes that we facilitate we look at formal ways of introducing new ideas. When we work with the concept of the manager 'as a provider of a service of management to staff, who in turn provide a service to the customer', we ask each participant to explain this concept to the people they work with and then gain feedback from them, using the 'seven keys to success' questionnaire (see pages 63–64).[9] This process is helpful in two ways: it informs staff about a new way of managing, and also enables the participant to gain 360-degree feedback on their performance (see Figure 11).

Figure 11

360-DEGREE FEEDBACK

your manager

people you work with on specific projects

your colleagues

Feedback on your performance from

your staff

yourself

One of our participants described his management style as an 'old pair of slippers' – comfortable, familiar, and shaped to suit him. When he encountered the concept of the manager *as a provider of a service of management to staff, who in turn provide a service to the customer*, he felt both sceptical and uncomfortable, because it turned his traditional views of management upside down. Why put on a new pair of slippers when the old ones had not been worn out? How would his staff feel about his change of style? He felt that he was like his slippers – too old for changing.

The development programme he was participating in required that he gain 360-degree feedback from his staff. When he did this, he began to realise that his old slippers were worn and full of holes, and that his staff would actually welcome a new way of doing things.

SIGNAL: tell the appropriate people something about your development activity

Suzanne Leckie became aware of the need to spend time preparing the ground for self-development as a result of not sharing her reflections sufficiently with her partner, while she was engaged in formal self-development activity at work. She stresses the importance of alerting appropriate people at the very beginning and of sharing the new thoughts (and confusion) that can be part of our self-development with those close to you, at home and at work.

A participant left one of our courses filled with enthusiasm to make changes. He decided to involve all his family in planning what they wanted to do differently over the following 10 years.

He recognised that up until then he had been an emergent learner and taken jobs that had come up. Yet during the course he recognised that he had both the power and the incentive to get more of what he wanted by planning his future and making things happen. Awareness also grew that he would like to minimise the difference between his 'work self' and his 'home self' – in other words, enjoy himself much more at work. His family held a 'conference' in which everyone had a chance to say where they would like to be in 10 years' time, they discussed his future career within this framework.

Another participant returned home from a residential programme with vague feelings that she was no longer happy with what she was doing with her life. It was difficult for her initially to put these feelings into words because she did not know what she needed to change – she just knew that she had to take time out to explore her disquiet. When she told her husband about this he panicked, thinking she wanted a divorce. She was able to explain that this was not the case and that she wanted to work with him on these issues so that they could develop a joint purpose for the future.

MANOEUVRE: *choose the best method, release the handbrake, and have fun*

We can approach self-development from many perspectives. Our risk-taking can lead us to new places, some planned, some unexpected. We hope that the next few chapters will provide you with a map, and that you will enjoy your journey of self-development.

In brief

This chapter helps us to focus on how to prepare ourselves for a self-development programme. The metaphor of the learner driver is used to help us develop our thoughts.

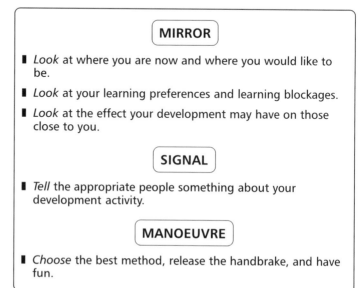

MIRROR

■ *Look* at where you are now and where you would like to be.

■ *Look* at your learning preferences and learning blockages.

■ *Look* at the effect your development may have on those close to you.

SIGNAL

■ *Tell* the appropriate people something about your development activity.

MANOEUVRE

■ *Choose* the best method, release the handbrake, and have fun.

References

1   LECKIE S. 'Preparing the Ground for Self-development'. Unpublished paper, Sheffield Hallam University. (1995)

2   WHITAKER V. 'Mentoring and Letting Go'. Proceedings of the First European Mentoring Conference, Sheffield Hallam University. (1994)

3   SCHEIN E. *Process Consultation*. Reading MA, Addison Wesley. (1969)

4   WHITAKER V. *Managing People*. London, HarperCollins. (1994)

5   STRAANGARD F. *NLP Made Visual*. Copenhagen, Connector. (1981)

6   PIERING T. *Mastery: A technology for excellence and personal evolution*. Sierra Madre CA, Sun West. (1988)

7   MEGGINSON D. 'Planned and emergent learning'. *Executive Development*, Vol. 7, No.6. (1994)

8   MEGGINSON D. 'Planned and emergent learning: consequences for development'. Sheffield, British Academy of Management Conference. (1995)

9   WHITAKER V. *Managing People*. London, HarperCollins. (1994)

4

The Self-Development Process

Introduction

Up to this point we have been addressing self-development from the viewpoint both of individuals who are developing themselves as well as managers and professionals who are helping other individuals to develop. Over this and the next chapter we explore the setting-up of schemes for self-development. These are typically established by HR (human resource) professionals, with or without the assistance of outside consultants.

Development-oriented line managers are also beginning to make the running in setting up these processes as the core development activity for their area of responsibility. So, whatever your responsibility or role, Chapters 4 and 5 offer you an approach to setting up a self-development process for a number of people.

We used the word 'process' in the previous sentence because we want to discourage you from thinking of self-development as a product, programme, or scheme. There are no 'right' answers here. We describe our frameworks and the components within them as specifically as we can – not to encourage you to create a new development orthodoxy by copying what we do, but to encourage you to find a process that makes sense to *you* in the circumstances of *your* organisation or group.

In this chapter we concentrate on principles, frameworks,

and the briefest introduction to the components. These are illustrated using the process adopted by Texaco Ltd. In Chapter 5 we spell out in greater detail what we have learnt about each of these components.

Principles

In designing schemes we bear in mind the following principles:

∎ There is no right answer.
∎ Voluntarism.
∎ Keep the culture in mind.
∎ Focus on the business case.
∎ Increase the capability for self-development.

There is no right answer

As self-development moves centre stage into organisations' development efforts, it is tempting to create a formula or product. 'We tried this there and it worked, so it will work for you' would be an expression of this view. We resist such temptations on the grounds that each organisation's context and purposes are somewhat different from all others.

There is also something inherently developmental in working with a group of people in an organisation to create something that is their own and to which they can relate. It may be a way of connecting with individuals in HR departments who have not hitherto been touched by developmental thinking. It may equally be a way of connecting with stakeholders in the client group and enhancing their understanding so that they can become informed advocates of the process. We find that the creativity and insight of individuals in these teams help us to learn new things and re-invent, and develop, our understanding of self-development processes.

Voluntarism

Many of the organisations we work with are used to training and development initiatives that are rolled out to all members of a particular population. This, they argue, is the only way to ensure that we spread the effect that we seek to the whole group. If we do not do this, they go on to say, then the people who need it most will be the ones who do not show up. In spite of these arguments we tend to support the view that the process should include the maximum voluntarism that can be borne. This issue is a real dilemma, however, and both sides have a case.

On the one hand, we have many experiences of people saying:

> I was the fiercest critic of this self-development stuff when it started, but I realise that there is a lot to it, and I needed the prod to get me to see how others saw me. I now recognise that there were things I wasn't as good at as I thought I was.

These individuals are going to miss this chance if there is not an element of pressure to attend.

On the other hand, we have also seen the surge of energy and commitment that comes from individuals and groups committing themselves to continuing a development process when they feel they have a real option to stop.

Voluntarism in many organisations' cultures means that only a small fraction of those invited feel strong enough to refuse, but the evidence which these individuals provide that voluntarism exists, can be a spur to all the others who do go along with the process.

One way of dealing with the dilemma is to say, 'The self-development scheme is voluntary, but doing nothing about your development is not an option; so if for any reason you do not want to get involved with what we offer, make a case that you are taking other steps to develop yourself.'

Keep the culture in mind

The culture in organisations affects how people regard self-development. We assess the culture of an organisation as we commence working with our clients and then feed back our assessment to the people we are working with. One medium-sized UK subsidiary of a foreign-owned company felt like a vast multinational – committees, consultation, procedures, and protocols for everything. We found ourselves immersed in these and frustrated by them. It was not until we looked inside, and realised that we were talking about an organisation with fewer than 2,000 employees in the UK, that we could help our clients step out of the constitutionalist, mandarin style, and move the process forwards with more urgency and purpose than we had managed up to that point. (David Casey has a model of 'taking in from self' and 'taking in from the group or organisation', 'making sense' of it, and then 'intervening', which beautifully describes this process.[1])

Focus on the business case

As advocates of self-development we are often tempted to see ourselves as guerrilla fighters for the individual in organisations where this focus seems lacking. However, our experience is that we do not do individuals any favours by shifting attention away from business issues.

Most organisation members want their development to further the development of the organisation. If it fails to do so, not only do they expect that the initiative will be short-lived, but it may also feel isolating and dangerous. It may be argued that living through isolation and danger is a highly developmental process, and indeed it can be. One may also argue that the interests of the majority of self-developers are best served by setting up a strong dialogue between individual needs and organisational imperatives.

Our experience also indicates that, by allowing this tension to be played out, self-development initiatives are often strengthened, and that it moves them in the direction of organisational development.

In one company in which we were working we used Ed Schein's framework of the cultural iceberg. We encouraged participants to explore current assumptions at work in their organisation as well as suggest others with which they would like to replace them. They presented their views to their line manager and their managing director, which turned out to be quite a chastening experience. It also built shared understandings and a commitment to organisation-wide action to address assumptions and behaviours within the organisation. Some of the current assumptions of which people were critical were that only managers make decisions, that the messenger can be shot, and that things are done a certain way because they are always done that way. Participants in the programme, however, wanted more positive assumptions to be adopted, eg that people's experience is listened to and valued, and that people are encouraged.

Increase the capability for self-development

It helps to increase the capability for self-development in organisations if a wide range of stakeholders is involved in the programme design. External staff can be used for their depth of experience, but the involvement of internal HR and line staff as facilitators or planners can be highly developmental. Working in partnership increases ownership of the programme and ensures that it is linked to other development initiatives within the organisation.

Involving HR professionals whose experience has not so far included working with development initiatives can be challenging and rewarding. Encounters, debates, and skill-development processes with experienced and new facilitators have led to periods of rapid learning for both parties.

Frameworks for self-development

Having said that there is no one right model for self-development processes in organisations, it would be contradictory just to present a list and say that if you want to do it right then you need to include all the elements in it. Some initiatives are more comprehensive than others, but our feeling is that each component needs to be examined to see whether, in its particular circumstances, it adds 'learning and development value'. We have therefore listed in Table 4 a comprehensive set of components that we have incorporated into self-development processes and included a brief description of what is involved, along with the desired effect on the nature and focus of the process.

Table 4 on pages 50–51 illustrates how each initiative will tilt a self-development process towards one of a number of emphases. These are:

■ individual self-development
■ team development
■ work performance
■ a learning community
■ peer support and challenge
■ connection to organisation goals
■ interorganisational learning
■ learning from work
■ widening the learning.

Putting the components together – an example

Texaco Ltd's self-development process, Mpower ('empower'), illustrates how, for one company, we made a selection from the range of options in Table 4 to create a self-development process customised to the needs of that organisation. Texaco also runs a sister process called GMpower, for general managers, which has a somewhat different design. The overall structure of Mpower is shown in Figure 12 on page 52.

Table 4

SELF-DEVELOPMENT PROCESS COMPONENTS

Self-development component	Features	Effect
Diagnostic instruments (eg learning styles, team roles)	Questionnaire that gives individuals feedback about their self-perception or about how others see them.	Enhances realistic self-image; encourages focus on individual self-development.
360-degree feedback	Feedback to individuals of results of diagnostic instruments completed about them by others; can be followed with a team meeting.	Develops personal agenda for behaviour change; directs attention at the working of the manager's team.
Development agreement	Specifies where individuals have been, where they are, and where they want to be.	Encourages thinking ahead about personal development or work performance.
Initial workshop	Introduces self-development concepts and skills; establishes learning sets.	Builds a learning community wider than the learning set; enables business objectives to be linked to the development effort.
Learning sets	Groups of no more than seven that meet periodically to support and challenge individuals' development activities at work.	Emphasises peer support and challenge; encourages focus on learning rather than single-minded attention to the task itself.
Half-way workshops	Review of progress and renewal of commitment.	Encourages connection to organisational goals and dialogue with senior stakeholders. *(continued opposite)*

Table 4 (continued)
SELF-DEVELOPMENT PROCESS COMPONENTS

Self-development component	Features	Effect
Attachments	Short periods of secondment to other organisations.	Encourages outward perspective and interorganisational learning.
Action learning project	Encourages the testing of personal development against the reality of demanding work tasks.	Focuses on learning in the context of work.
Final workshop	Opportunity for participants to summarise their learning and to set a direction for the next cycle; senior management can use this to support continuing development and widen the effect to include others.	Emphasises cyclical and continuous development; puts a line under the development so far; encourages relating the learning to the organisation's goals.
Organisation learning day	Brings together those involved in self-development from diverse parts of the organisation.	Encourages widespread learning; focuses the culture change efforts of individual schemes.
Large group intervention	Uses development processes to address organisational issues.	Reduces elitism by involving a wide range of people.

Figure 12

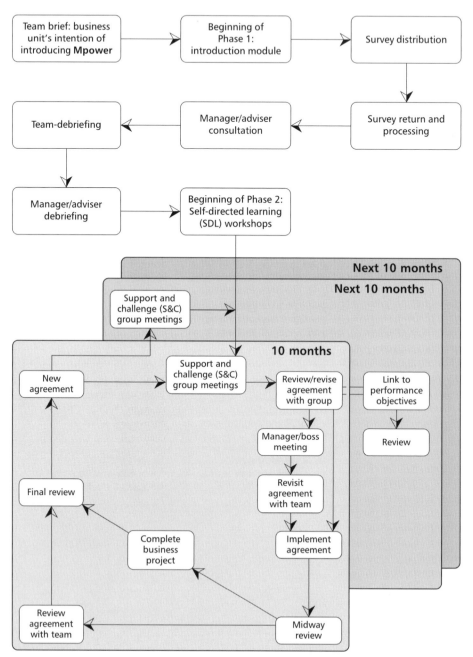

AN OVERVIEW OF 'MPOWER'

The first part of Texaco to offer Mpower was the company's wholesale and supply (W & S) business unit. W & S is concerned with the storage, distribution, and transportation of refined products and their sale to large customers. The general manager of W & S volunteered to pilot Mpower. His goal was to encourage his managers to increase their proactivity and to become more business-focused, because W & S was becoming a profit centre for the first time. Many of the managers in W & S worked in isolated depots, and they were older and of longer service than was the norm in Texaco.

The following is an account of why the components of Mpower were chosen and of the way they were structured to achieve the desired results. The account also describes where they did not wholly achieve these results, and what we learnt from the process.

Team brief and introduction module

The managers were introduced to the Mpower process. It was illustrated how 360-degree feedback was related to leadership practices that characterised effective managers in Texaco.

Survey distribution, return and processing

Texaco had an established relationship with an organisation that distributed surveys and trained internal HR staff and external consultants involved in the rest of the Mpower programme as advisers who would feed back the data from the surveys. Some advisers felt that this was a challenging step for them and sought extra support through observing a more experienced facilitator run the process. They then did their first cycle as adviser, with observation and feedback from their experienced colleague.

Manager/adviser consultation

These two-hour meetings involved making sense of the 360-degree feedback and creating a plan for handling a team-debriefing session, at which the data would be explored with the manager's direct reports.

Team-debriefing

The team meetings were often the first opportunity that managers had of receiving focused feedback from their staff. Many of them approached the process with a degree of trepidation, but the outcomes, although sometimes challenging, were almost universally seen as constructive and useful.

Manager/adviser-debriefing

Managers had the opportunity of having a one-hour debriefing with their consultant, and many of them took advantage of this. Most found it useful.

Self-directed learning (SDL) workshops

The 24 managers involved in W & S went to one of two of these workshops, so there were roughly 12 at each. At the workshops they learnt something about setting a 'development agreement', and they formed themselves into learning sets. The workshops lasted two days, and one proved more successful than the other. At the second workshop many participants complained that it was too long and that they did not need to prepare development agreements – they just wanted to get on. At one level, these concerns reflected the 'can do', action-orientation of many of the managers. It may also have been the case that the workshop was overegging the introductory process, because managers had become used to thinking about their own development as a result of going through the 360-degree feedback processes.

Support and challenge group meetings

Following the SDL workshops, four support and challenge (S & C) groups began meeting, facilitated by members of

Texaco's HRM staff. These facilitators, who became known as the M4 group, decided that the two days of training that they had received before the SDL workshops were only a foundation. They therefore set up regular half-day development workshops, which mirrored the processes they helped the managers go through. The HRM facilitators had an external facilitator for these meetings.

Midway review

Just before the midway review, a new general manager was appointed to W & S. HR and external facilitators met with him and he agreed to use the midway session as an opportunity to brief the managers on his strategic direction and to explore with them how Mpower would contribute to this. The event therefore included review, recommitment, and reconnection and the S & C groups committed themselves to continuing. Two groups accepted new members from among the new managers who had joined W & S and wanted to get together with an existing group.

Additional learning activities

As well as continuing their S & C group meetings, the groups were offered additional sources of support, including:

- *a development-agreement coaching session*. Many managers had been reluctant to commit themselves to paper in preparing their development agreement, so this facility was offered to help them prepare a written account of their goals.
- *individual development budgets*. These were negotiated to enable individuals to purchase their own training or to pool the budgets and use them for collaborative purposes.
- *business projects*. Offered on a voluntary basis, these were taken up with enthusiasm by some groups and avoided equally forcefully by others.
- *managing-yourself techniques*. Derived from Pedler and

Boydell's *Managing Yourself* (see page 10, reference no. 6), these tools were made available for individuals or groups.

∎ *insight workshops*. These were offered to whole S & C groups to explore and to work on with colleagues concerning their leadership practices and styles.

Final workshop

There was a one-day workshop to celebrate achievements, crystallise learning, evaluate effects, set new directions, and introduce others to the process.

Each self-development programme has a life and purpose of its own; organisations that absorb one use each initiative as a springboard for the next, and ensure that what has been learnt from the first is incorporated into subsequent designs.

In brief

This chapter explores the setting up of schemes for self-development. Consider the extent to which it is appropriate for you to adopt the following principles:

∎ Create the design for the situation rather than buy it off the shelf or simply repeat what worked elsewhere.

∎ Participation should be voluntary.

∎ Respond to the culture without just being absorbed into it.

∎ Balance business needs with individual needs.

∎ Build alliances by involving a wide range of stakeholders in design and facilitation.

Consider also which of the following components you wish to include in your self-development process (you will get further details on each of them in the next chapter):

- diagnostic instruments to help participants develop a truly realistic self-image
- 360-degree feedback to develop a personal agenda for change
- development agreements to encapsulate a plan for change
- an initial workshop to build a learning community, group skills, and business case
- learning sets to provide support and challenge in pursuing development objectives
- half-way workshops to connect with organisational goals and dialogue with stakeholders
- attachments to encourage outward perspective and interorganisational learning
- action learning projects to focus on learning at and through work
- a final workshop to draw a line under the process and to lead into the next cycle.

Reference

1   CASEY D. *Managing Learning in Organisations*. Buckingham, Open University. (p25) (1993)

5

Creating a Self-Development Programme

In this chapter we describe a range of activities that could form part of a self-development programme. They are listed under the following headings:

- know yourself
- make a plan
- individual tools
- learning sets
- working with the organisation.

Know yourself

Peter Senge uses the image of two hands stretching an elastic band to illustrate how we can know ourselves accurately.[1] The hand at the top represents vision, the one at the bottom a clear picture of current reality. Being clear about both of these provides the tension that leads to learning. In this section we deal with the bottom hand: knowing where you stand now.

Scott Inglis uses a striking phrase to denote this bottom hand.[2] He suggests that when we start on the path of development we need 'an Extraordinarily Realistic Self Image (ERSI)'. How might we form such a picture of ourselves?

One way is to ask. Another 10 ways are to 'Ask, ask, ask, ask, ask, ask, ask, ask, ask, ask.' There is no substitute for openness to the views of others. Many people have been delighted by the feedback they received: they did not realise that their staff, managers, and colleagues valued their work.

Yet we do not have to accept others' views willy-nilly. There might be some people whom we could ask who would take a spiteful delight in giving us information in a hurtful way. There might be others who, to use the analysts' jargon, would project onto us their own inadequacies. Nonetheless, even malicious or deluded data about us may have some relevance; and we can extract from it what is valuable and let go the rest.

> One way to gather data from others is to ask 10 people who know you how they see you performing at present, and what they think you need to do next to develop yourself. Write down your understanding of what they say and then check it with them to see if you have captured the essence of their message. Review the 10 messages and see if you can discern a pattern. What are the four or five big messages that arise from this feedback? Save this information to combine with metrics from any questionnaires that you might use. Then take it to your self-development group or learning set and seek help from people there in converting it into a personal development plan (see pages 65–70).

Another way of gaining feedback is to use a variety of questionnaires.

Feedback from questionnaires

Some of the commonest measures that people use to assess themselves at the start of a self-development process are:

■ the Myers-Briggs Type Indicator (MBTI)
■ the McBer Management Styles Questionnaire (MSQ)

■ Boydell and Pedler's Self-managing Climate Questionnaire
■ Honey and Mumford's Learning Style Questionnaire (LSQ)
■ Belbin's Team Role Inventory
■ Margerison and McCann's Team Management Index

Sources for each of these are given in Chapter 7. Their uses in self-development are described below.

The Myers-Briggs Type Indicator (MBTI)

This psychometric test assesses four dimensions of personality, (based on a self-report questionnaire) developed from C. G. Jung's model of personality. They measure whether:

■ energy is directed outward (extroversion) or inward (introversion)
■ perception relies on actual experience (sensing) or on possibilities and inspiration (intuiting)
■ decisions are based on the logic of the situation (thinking) or on human values and needs (feeling)
■ the preferred lifestyle is planned (judging) or spontaneous (perceiving).

These dimensions yield 16 four-letter type descriptions. These are charmingly described as specifying 16 ways of being a splendid human being, so the model is not designed to help you develop or improve your personality (a fruitless task), but to come to terms with it, and to see the possible strengths that you have to offer.

The McBer Management Styles Questionnaire (MSQ)

This questionnaire enables you to describe yourself, or to get feedback from others, against six possible styles. These styles and their primary objectives are:

- coercive – seeks immediate compliance
- authoritative – provides long-term direction and vision
- affiliative – creates harmony
- democratic – builds commitment through consensus
- pacesetting – accomplishes immediate tasks to high standards
- coaching – long-term employee development.

The MSQ, unlike the Myers-Briggs, is 'normative', in that some styles are shown by research to be generally more effective, especially the affiliative, democratic, and coaching. However, McBer also has a questionnaire that measures managerial situations, and can suggest that a different range of the six styles might be suitable for a particular context.

Materials are available that specify the competencies linked with each of the styles and make suggestions as to how to develop them. For example, one of the competencies associated with the coaching style is 'Establish professional and developmental goals', and part of the advice for developing this is to 'Ask your employees to project some long-term professional goals for themselves'.

Boydell and Pedler's Self-managing Climate Questionnaire

This short questionnaire from Mike Pedler and Tom Boydell offers a way of assessing the climate that a manager is creating in his or her own part of an organisation.[3] One participant in a self-development programme for senior managers in local authorities in the north-east of England used the questionnaire to examine the climate in his own department and benchmarked it against other departments. He also sought the views of his chief officer, colleagues, and the chief executive, and thus raised some very interesting questions not just for developing his own patch, but for the whole authority as well.

The questionnaire has just 10 questions exploring:

- the physical environment
- learning resources
- encouragement to learn
- communications
- rewards
- conformity
- the value placed on ideas
- practical help available
- warmth and support
- standards.

Honey and Mumford's Learning Styles Questionnaire (LSQ)

The 80 items in the LSQ give a reading on your preferred learning style. They address your preferences as to the four quadrants of the learning cycle that we introduced in Chapter 1 (see page 2). Linking our work to Honey and Mumford's terms, the four quadrants are described as:

- activist (do something)
- reflector (think about it)
- theorist (make sense of it)
- pragmatist (do it differently).

There is no particular best style here, although Honey and Mumford suggest that balanced learning requires an ability to operate all the way round the cycle. This can offer an agenda in choosing learning goals and plans that enables you to practise your least preferred styles.

Belbin's Team Role Inventory and Margerison and McCann's Team Management Index

Both of these measures allow you to examine which of a range of possible contributions you tend to make to a team. Again there are no right or wrong answers.

However, team roles can be changed and developed with practice, and both frameworks allow you to choose areas for development.

360-degree feedback

Nowadays, rather than just relying on feedback from direct reports to enrich the appraisal of managers, many companies propose gathering feedback from the appraisee and his or her peers as well: hence the term 360-degree feedback. Indeed we have seen some companies also gathering feedback from suppliers and customers, thus making the feedback 540 degrees – implying a sphere rather than a circle!

Megginson and Pedler, describe a process of gaining 360-degree feedback that was called the 'Upward Feedback Process' in BP Exploration (BPX).[4] The present authors were both facilitators during this process, which was introduced throughout the organisation over a six-month period and which assisted both individuals and the organisation to function more effectively.

In organisations like BPX, where key competencies for excellent performance have been identified, managers can seek feedback against these criteria. If an organisation has not created such criteria then there are models that can be used.

Vivien's research into the manager as a provider of a service of management to staff, led to the creation of just such a framework – the 'seven keys to success' – which can be used to gather 360-degree feedback.[5] The 'seven keys to success' has two slightly different questionnaires: one for the manager him- or herself and one for others providing feedback. It seeks respondents' views on how important each of the characteristics is and how much it is being manifested by the individual (see Figure 13 on page 64).

Figure 13

THE SEVEN KEYS TO SUCCESS

1 Clarity
- Provide clarity in all your written and verbal communication.
- Show consistency regarding necessary confidentiality.
- Maintain effective systems of information-sharing.

2 Customers
- Recognise that you provide a service of management to both external and internal customers.
- Design systems and structures to serve your customers/patients/students.
- Define quality in terms of customer satisfaction and gain constant customer feedback.

3 Confidence
- Increase the self-confidence of your staff through delegation and the provision of continual constructive feedback.
- Have the self-confidence to recognise, acknowledge, and sort out difficult situations.
- Seek new ways of doing things – take risks and do things differently.

4 Co-operation
- Agree, and work to, shared ways of operating with your staff.
- Ensure that men and women are working effectively together.
- Develop long-term customer–supplier relationships.

5 Creativity
- Use mistakes as learning experiences to improve service.
- Encourage and reward initiative and innovation by your staff.
- Develop your team and gain ideas through shared problem-solving.

6 Commitment
- Value your staff and recognise their different talents.
- Ensure that you and your staff are committed to acting responsibly – hold people accountable for what they do.
- Show commitment to the goals of your team and the purpose of your organisation.

7 Choices
- Recognise that you can influence outcomes, because you are in control of your response to events.
- Regard issues not as puzzles that have one right answer but as problems that have a range of solutions.
- Transform problems into opportunities.

Summary

It is important when starting out on a process of self-development to develop a clear image of yourself. Asking others how they see you helps you do this. Questionnaires and 360-degree feedback are useful in this process.

Make a plan

Armed with feedback from others, a set of psychometric data from some of the sources outlined above, and the results of 360-degree feedback you will be in a position to develop a truly realistic self-image. What you can do with this data is the subject of this section.

Framework for a development agreement

A development agreement is a document that you produce to record your intentions for your own development: it is an agreement with yourself. It is also okay to change your agreement. In fact, one of the participants on our employment department programme said that his most important discovery was that *changing* goals was as crucial a developmental step as *achieving* the goals he set. It is the difference between doing things right and doing right things, or the distinction that Chris Argyris makes between single-loop learning and double-loop learning.[6] Of course, changing goals is on its own not enough. Action must then be taken. However, having a 'right' direction for action is a crucial first step.

Particular formats

Melanie Hollinshead, one of the talented facilitators on the BP upward feedback process with which we were involved, introduced us to the idea of the 'design on the back'. If you do not like any of the formats we suggest you can always turn the page over and use the design on the back, which means (assuming the page is not printed on both sides) use a blank sheet or make up your own columns and headings.

One effective format for development agreements is provided by the five questions asked by Ian Cunningham.[7] The five questions are:

■ Where have I been?

■ Where am I now?

■ Where do I want to be?

■ How shall I get there?

■ How shall I know when I arrive?

Rennie Fritchie has added two further, powerful questions that could perhaps best be inserted between the second and third questions above:[8]

■ What kind of human being do I want to be?

■ What do I want to do with my life?

> Before rushing on with your reading of this book, spend as long as you can answering some or all of these seven questions. Make a note of any major points or new thoughts you come up with.

This kind of format can provide a valuable framework for voluntary self-exploration. In some organisations and for some people, however, it may seem too much. In thoughtful, reflective climates it works well, but in hustling, can-do organisations it may be rejected.

Continuous Professional Development (CPD)

The IPD's own CPD framework, which David has been using since 1992, has a similar set of questions, with some useful and detailed subquestions. The headings that he uses are: 'preparation' and 'plan':

Preparation

■ What do I do well in my present job?

■ What could I do better?

■ Where and in what roles do I see my future?
■ What new knowledge and skills shall I need?
■ What support might I need from colleagues?
■ What constraints or problems do I foresee?
■ What resources are available to me?
■ What development methods should I use?

Plan

■ Work activities as source of learning.
■ Professional activities.
■ Courses and conferences.
■ Reading.
■ Self-directed and informal activities.
■ Groups.

Create 12 goals for yourself for the coming year. Do this by brainstorming 40 or so possible goals and then choose no more than 12 to be the priorities. For each goal set up a chart specifying the:

■ goal
■ method of achieving
■ contacts for help
■ constraints
■ events.

David's self-development file sits comfortably on the hard disk of one of our computers and, every now and then, throughout each year, he updates his goals. At the beginning of each new year he thoroughly reviews the goals he set and then creates a new set of 12 goals for the coming year. Keeping the same document over a number of years helps to keep one aware of how one has done in the past.

The IPD's new computer-based format was sent to every member of the institute in late 1995 as a disk with their copies of *People Management*; it is an improvement on the previous paper format, in that it creates a structure that is user-friendly and offers prompts for thinking about one's development. It is also delightfully easy to update – to add further details about progress towards goals established earlier, or to add new goals that follow on from those earlier ones. The new format offers a range of helpful activities to contribute towards achieving developmental goals; it is possible to incorporate these into your plan by pointing and clicking on-screen. On the other hand, if you have personal ways of developing yourself that are not included, or you want to be more specific about the methods in the IPD list, then it is easy to add your own details.

The IPD plans to make completion of the CPD process obligatory for members. This highlights one of the deep dilemmas in development. In Chapter 2 we made out a case for voluntarism; all the same, we acknowledge the imperative on a professional body to seen to be require members to update themselves. Peter Honey has made a case for making development compulsory on the grounds that it usefully formalises the process of learning from experience.[9] He bases his argument on four assumptions:

▮ Learning from experience is too important to be left to chance.

▮ People rarely do more than they need to.

▮ 'Good' behaviour should never be assumed.

▮ In most organisations, upward deference is rife.

A final word on CPD: in the Institute of Management's report *Survival of the Fittest*, Neville Benbow found that 'More than 80 per cent of respondents believed that CPD will become increasingly important for managers.'

A question that immediately arises once a format has been found is, 'How can I be sure that the goals that I have set for myself are the right ones?' An answer lies in testing out your own thoughts with some trusted advisers. Who might these advisers be? Our list would include:

- your line manager
- a trusted colleague
- trusted staff
- friends
- mentor(s)
- (crucially) a self-development group or learning set.

Using a self-development group or learning set

One of the first tasks of new learning sets is to help members to validate, and feel confident about, their development agreement. We explore the workings of groups that enable them to perform this function later in this chapter; for now, it is worth saying that the advantages of clarifying the agreement with the help of the set are that:

- it gives groups a concrete task early in their life
- it provides tangible opportunities for helping and sharing perspectives
- it gives a chance to practise the skills of giving and receiving feedback
- it gets a set of alternative perspectives on the development agreement, which enables you to choose among them and still retain ownership of the agreement as yours.

Preparing a development agreement

- Find a format that you can use for your development agreement.
- Remember there is always the option of 'the other side of the page'.
- Make time to answer the questions that your framework poses.
- Spend individual time first, even if you have the offer of help from others, and consider the issues raised in Chapter 3.

- Record your first thoughts on each section of your agreement.

- Meet with some other people you trust and seek their support in developing your agreement.

- Tell other people who are important to you – family, colleagues, your manager – about what goals you have set. This will increase your commitment to action and at the same time increase the consequences of not achieving your goals – the 'pressure cooker' approach.

Summary

Individuals can be helped to set, and hold to, a direction in their own development by preparing a development plan. The precise format of this plan is less important than the individual's degree of commitment to it. Continuous professional development is increasingly recognised as a requirement for managers and professionals, and it requires the individual to prepare a plan. Learning sets can help individuals to prepare such plans.

Individual tools
Learning logs

A key tool for deepening our individual learning is the learning log. This is a deceptively simple device for chewing over a bit of experience and squeezing the learning out of it. Someone once said he thought that an unconsidered life was not worth leading. Proponents of the learning log would agree with this. A learning log is shown in Figure 14, opposite, with suggestions for its use.

The learning log is such a fine tool for learning because it encourages us to work round the learning cycle (see Chapter 1 page 2). The 'event' has been an opportunity for us to *do something*. The 'what happened' section gives us an opportunity to *think about it*. The 'conclusions' part is where we *make sense of it*, and the action part is where we explore how we will *do it differently*.

Figure 14

LEARNING LOG

Activity: Logging learning
Identify a recent experience that seemed significant at the time, but that you have not chewed over to any great extent since. Give it a name at the top of the log.

Write down as factually as you can *what happened*. This can include what others did, but pay particular attention to your part in the events. Include your feelings and thoughts at the time, but do not attempt any analysis at this stage.

Now write your *conclusions*. These will answer the question, 'So what?' This section offers you a chance to make sense of the experience. How does what happened – and particularly what you did – relate to what you know about people, groups, or organisations? Does it lead you to change your view about what you think you know? Does what you know offer you any thoughts as to what you might have done differently?

Finally, record what *action* you will take. This could be things specifically related to this event, or be about how you might behave differently in similar circumstances, or what you might do to develop yourself to handle this sort of situation differently in the future.

Event

What happened

Conclusions

Action

Biography work

Another tool for self-development stands right at the opposite end of the scale from the learning log. If the log looks at a particular incident, then biography work takes as its focus the whole of our lives. The lifeline that we described in Chapter 3 (see page 33) is a good starter-exercise for working on your biography. It offers a perspective on the movement of a life over time, and allows for a projection of a desired future state. Many models of career-planning take a biographical perspective, encouraging self-developers to examine what motives have driven their career in the past and what motives will be the drivers in the future. These motives are referred to by a number of names, 'career anchors' or 'career drivers' being two of the best known. They may include:

- income
- power
- achievement
- position
- security
- recognition
- family
- community
- profession
- living out values
- political contribution
- spiritual life.

Consider the 12 motives listed above and ask yourself
which have been dominant in the last period of your
life. Then ask yourself what order you would like to
manifest itself in the next period of your life. Note
which changes are the biggest in order, both up and
down. Then ask yourself the following questions:

∎ What am I going to have to change in myself to
  bring about this re-prioritisation?

∎ Who else will be affected by my making these
  changes?

∎ What do I have to do to ensure that these changes
  will be experienced positively by these other
  people?

Another exercise we have found especially useful in
biography work is called the U-process. The steps you
take go down one side of a U, across the bottom, and up
the other side. They are outlined in Figure 15.

Looking first at your past, write down under 'Phenomena'
the key events and turning-points in your life. In 'Phases'
divide these up into time periods – give each period a
name. Under 'Themes' note what underlying patterns or
aspirations appear in your life so far. At the 'Current reality'
step ask yourself what questions and issues are coming
your way and what the overall picture of your life is so
far, and consider the people in your consciousness who
provide a role model or have a message for you. Moving
to the future, list under the Visions and intentions, record
the misachieved aspirations you are in touch with. One
way of developing 'Strategies and options' (the next step)
is to identify areas that you want to change, list alternative
actions, and specify your choice. Finally, under 'First steps',
list the specific actions that will get you going on this
goal. (See also Tom Boydell and Malcolm Leary's book
in this series, *Identifying Training Needs*, London, IPD,
1996, pp 151–154.)

Figure 15

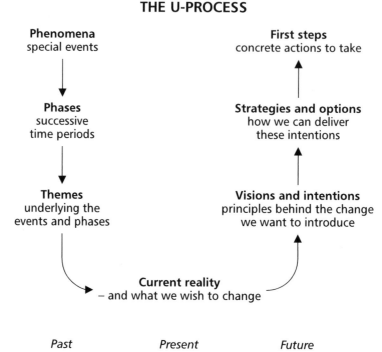

THE U-PROCESS

Phenomena
special events

Phases
successive
time periods

Themes
underlying the
events and phases

First steps
concrete actions to take

Strategies and options
how we can deliver
these intentions

Visions and intentions
principles behind the change
we want to introduce

Current reality
– and what we wish to change

Past   *Present*   *Future*

Self-development texts and tapes

There is a huge number of books and tapes designed to help you develop yourself. Among the best of the texts are Mike Pedler and Tom Boydell's *Managing Yourself*, (2nd edition, HarperCollins, London, 1994), and Mike Pedler, John Burgoyne, and Tom Boydell's, *A Manager's Guide to Self-development*, (3rd edition, McGraw-Hill, Maidenhead, 1994). The best self-improvement tape we have come across is Jack Canfield's, *Self-esteem and Peak Performance*, available from Careertrack. We give a list of other useful books and resources in Chapter 7.

These sources contain a rich and valuable set of frameworks, diagnostics, and ideas for action. It is interesting to note, however, that Pedler and Boydell themselves found that the books used on their own were useful only for about 20 per cent of the people involved. Paradoxically, it seems, self-development works best with a group of fellow voyagers. We explore how to find and work with such a group in the next section.

Summary

To get into self-development and get moving in your life it is valuable to explore a range of development activities. Among the ones we suggest in this section are learning logs and biography work, including the U-process and self-development tapes and texts. We recommend that you use a number of these as an adjunct to any other self-development process you may be involved in.

Learning sets

Learning sets are a core component of self-development. Having a group of 'comrades in adversity' to support, but also, sometimes, to challenge, our learning and problem-solving is at the core of Reg Revans' method of action learning. In his method, the central task of individual set members is a major work task that they have taken on. They are charged not only with successfully completing the task but also with learning from it.

This approach was taken up by advocates of self-development groups. Here, however, the big work task has been replaced by a task of developing the self. These groups are also called self-directed or self-managed, and there are nuances of meaning between the different types. Perhaps the main reason for the perpetuation of these different 'brands' is that they represent markers put down by various authors in this area who lay claim to a unique part of the action. For this reason, these subtle distinctions need detain us no longer.

The purpose, membership, and facilitation of these groups are of central importance to the successful pursuit of self-development, and is the concern of the rest of this section.

Principles of learning sets (self-development groups)

The groups are founded on a number of principles:

- that we learn best when supported and challenged by others

- that it is easier to accept feedback from people we consider our peers rather than from those who have a different role, or from people who may be seen as superior in some way

- that, when time is shared and everyone has equitable access to the full attention of the rest of the group, it becomes easy to give full attention to others when it is their individual turn

- that 'helping' does not necessarily mean 'offering advice' – because we know more about our own situation than anyone else does; so the best help is often a penetrating question or a suggestion to be considered

- that maintaining the discipline required to sustain these purposes can be helped by a skilled facilitator.

In order to succeed, learning sets require:

- purpose
- process
- passion.

These three requirements do not necessarily remain unaltered throughout the life of the set. They need to be addressed at the start of the group's life, and attended to from time to time as it evolves.

Purpose

Purpose can come from three sources:

- the programme of self-development
- the learning set's deliberations
- the individual learners.

Specified purposes for self-development programmes include, obviously, some element of developing the individual. They may also include (and it is desirable that they should) an element of contributing to organisational purposes. Each set often spends some useful time early in its life considering its own purpose. It is not necessary to be alarmed if these conversations are anarchic and lead to objectives that go against those of the company or the programme. In our experience sets that are encouraged to explore their own purpose are highly responsible about how they define it. In fact we have known cases where they are seen as too conservative and company focused by senior managers sponsoring self-development, who wish to encourage a thorough-going commitment to personal growth as a prerequisite for any positive change in the organisation.

Process

The processes that enable groups to work well together are not complicated (see pages 78 – 79). Nonetheless they are important, and we have encountered too many groups that have become unfocused and have faded out as a result of not keeping to the discipline of the stages we outline. The crucial component seems to be that of allowing everyone to have their own time on their own issue. As Harvey Jackins, the founder of co-counselling, was fond of saying, 'Everyone, the whole world over, just wants to be listened to; the trouble is, so does everyone else!' Sharing time provides a process whereby each person receives this gift of time.

Passion

It is only when a set finds out what matters to each member, what is really hurting, and how practical help can be given and taken, that those in it develop a passion for the process. Typically for the first two or three meetings it is hard to hold people into the process. After a handful of meetings it is often hard to get them to stop. While we were finishing this chapter we were working with a high-flying senior manager who was attending a learning set meeting when she received an urgent call from her managing director to get back to work. It was impressive to see her manage the situation and her boss's perception of it so that she could continue doing what, to her, was the priority: developing the learning she needed to make an even bigger contribution to her organisation.

Typical stages in a group meeting

When groups work to the purposes and principles outlined above, they go through the following stages:

Check-in

Everybody in turn says something briefly about what has happened to them since the group last met. This can include how they have got on with the action they committed themselves to on the previous occasion; it can also involve unloading any pressing concerns or immediate baggage that they bring to the meeting with them (in south-east England this often concerns the state of the M25!).

Setting the agenda

Everybody then says what it is they want to explore with the group, and how long they think it might take. This and the previous stage are usually carried out without much discussion or questioning – otherwise the group get all too easily into the meat of the discussion without giving everyone a chance to 'check in' and bid for time. The group then agrees an agenda, which may be no more than the order in which people will have their time. Sometimes other items are added, reflecting an interest shared by two or more group members.

Individual time slots

This part will take up the bulk of the meeting. During

their time slot everybody summarises where they got to at the end of the previous meeting and what they said they would do by this meeting; they then report on how things have gone. It is useful not to get into praise or blame at this stage, because success or failure are of equal value as a source of potential learning. The group's task is to create a climate in which people report the situation as it is rather than boast of alleged success or excuse perceived failure. They then specify what it is they want from their time in the meeting and, unless this is challenged (in which case some re-contracting occurs), the group's task is then to help the individual to get what he or she wants. Someone needs to watch the distribution of time, because 'just a five-minute report' can easily become an impassioned, hour-long exploration of a surprising issue.

Check out
Summarising what each individual is committed to doing before the next set, and confirming the date, time, and place for that gathering.

Group frequency and duration

Groups can meet as often as once a fortnight or as seldom as once every two months. If meetings take place more frequently than once a fortnight individuals will not have much chance to act; if meetings occur with a gap of over two months then momentum and continuity can be lost.

The length of meetings depends on two factors:

■ the time between meetings – the greater the gap, the longer the meeting needs to be
■ the number in the group – less than 20 minutes for each person is not enough, so a group of six will require two hours' individual time, with perhaps half an hour for the topping-and-tailing process.

A less legitimate determinant of meeting length is the urgency of the demands on members of the group. The busier people are, the *more* valuable time away to reflect is. (This suggestion is easier to make in writing than carry through in practice!)

The facilitator/adviser's role

Given the points made above about the value of getting help from one's peers, what is the point of having a facilitator? Does it not negate the claim that what is going on in the group can be described as self-development?

In some senses it would be better, cheaper, and more developmental if the group was able to do without a facilitator. However, where this has been attempted in organisations – as in the early days of the corporate self-development scheme in Cable & Wireless – facilitators have been reintroduced to speed up the process of self-development.

In self-initiated groups, such as the facilitators group in ICL which started that company's exploration of self-development, or the male consultants' self-development group of which the only eligible author of this book has been a member for 10 years, no facilitator has been found necessary. Members of both these groups, possessed facilitating skills, so it sometimes felt as if everyone was a facilitator, but no one formally filled the role to the exclusion of their part as a member.

Summary

A core process in self-development is the support and challenge offered by one's peers in a small learning group. The group maximises benefit to its members by focusing on action and reflection. Facilitators, though not always essential, can greatly help a group's progress.

Working with the organisation
Connecting learning with work

Self-development often gives a buzz to the people involved but, in some organisations, this can cause nervousness among others – the staff, managers, or colleagues who work for the people getting that buzz. Those not involved can wonder: 'What are these people up to? Why are they going off and meeting with folk from other departments? Why do they seem to be more confident and better informed?' For many it is important that self-development initiatives be connected with the life and mission of the organisation.

A valuable way of doing this is to arrange workshops specifically for the purpose, so that people get to know what is going on. There are a number of ways of arranging such events, and a typical programme includes one or more of the following:

▐ action learning projects
▐ half-way workshops
▐ a workshop on the final day of the programme
▐ organisational learning days.

Making these links within organisations is crucial if you want your programme to facilitate organisational transformation. We shall describe each of these methods so you can assess which is most appropriate for your situation.

Action learning projects

Ian McGill and Liz Beattie emphasise that 'Action learning is based on reflection and action, and that the action side of the equation is called a project.'[10] They also say that 'Projects can be *anything* that a set member wishes to work on with the aid of the set process.' In this section we consider the kind of projects related to the business needs of an organisation. Many managers nowadays say that they have all the projects they need as a normal part of their work. The purpose of action learning projects is, however, to choose just one of these and use it as a source of accelerated reflective learning. By discussing the project in the learning set, participants gain a picture of themselves in action, which can be illuminating and challenging. It can lead them to attempt (and succeed at) activities that, without the set, they would not have attempted. Projects can be carried out either by individuals or by the set as a whole. Both options have their advantages. For people who do not have an obvious individual project, some criteria to consider are:

∎ Does the project it demonstrably link with the business strategy of the organisation?

∎ Does it offer an ongoing challenge requiring continuing exploration over several months?

∎ Does it matter, and is the participant 'for it'?

∎ Is there a sponsor (usually a senior manager) who is interested in progress and results?

∎ Is there a chance that the participant will be involved in the implementation?

If the answer to most of these questions is yes, then you have the basis for a successful action learning project.

Half-way workshops

These workshops are particularly useful if your programme includes several learning sets meeting over a period of time.

Once self-developers go off into learning sets it can become difficult for others to know what is going on. The contract of confidentiality is an important part of ensuring that the set works, but at the same time it is a barrier to transparency. To get round this problem, halfway workshops lasting a morning or afternoon provide a forum for people to disclose what they want to about the benefits they are experiencing. They can also be an opportunity for senior managers to learn about the initiative and to reinforce what they are seeking from the self-developers on the programme.

The workshops are arranged in this way: participants and their line managers are invited to an informal half-day event, which may include presentations and discussions. The emphasis of these events is on ensuring that senior managers are kept informed about their staff's progress. It is also a way of encouraging senior managers to provide appropriate support to enable their staff to achieve their personal development plan (PDP). In this way senior managers act as an 'umbrella', protecting their staff from additional pressures to enable them to have the time to focus on doing things differently.

In the Employment Service the half-way workshops in the head office development programme offered an opportunity for a member of the executive board to talk about the change to the Next Step agency, and about what that meant for everyone working there. It also opened up the channels for the three learning sets to say that they would like an opportunity to give their opinion on what was happening in the organisation to the executive board. This duly happened, and a constructive dialogue was set up in which representatives from the set met the board and expressed their views.

Final-day workshops

Final-day workshops are also an excellent opportunity for senior managers to connect with the development of participants and to learn from what they have achieved. Such workshops work particularly well if participants have been engaging in action learning and are giving presentations about their project and what they have achieved during the programme.

Mike Pupius, when he was Royal Mail's district head post-master in Sheffield, attended all the final-day workshops for his supervisors and superintendents. He was a model of excellent use of these workshops because he:

■ listened intently to each presentation

■ praised and encouraged participants for what they had achieved

■ linked what they were doing to the overall goals of the district and of Royal Mail

■ encouraged participants to apply their learning more widely by contacting others who might be interested in their findings.

Other programmes have used final-day workshops as both a way of looking back to highlight learning throughout the programme, and also as a way of looking to the future to develop another personal development programme for the year ahead.

Organisational learning days

Organisational learning days are particularly helpful when many different parts of an organisation are engaged in self-development.

Self-development is a relatively lonely process. Even in a learning set it is possible for participants to feel isolated and cut off from the rest of their organisation. Participants often say to us, 'It is all right in the set, but the kind of things we talk about here just aren't open for discussion elsewhere in the organisation.'

Organisational learning days create a norm for open, candid sharing, and enable those on the programme to take heart from the success of others. It can also be heartening to offer comradeship after hearing about the difficulties that other groups have encountered.

Roy Guy, Fiona Holden, and Phil Dickinson at ICL were three of the learning consultants in the company who had taken the initiative in setting up self-development in ICL businesses. They were also members of a self-initiated, self-development group that they had formed to support one another. They decided that, as a group, they would plan a day, during which managers and facilitators interested in self-development could come together and share what they had learnt and discuss what needed to be done. The day was considered as a success by those who participated. A memorable moment was when one of the line managers present, Austin Mullinder, said that his purpose in encouraging self-development in his own part of the company was to create a group of 'constructively unreasonable' people! (The organisational learning days continue at ICL in a variety of forms on a roughly annual basis.)

Summary

There is no contradiction between self-development and a contribution to strategic and business goals: they can feed off each other. Workshops at the half-way point in a programme and at the end can focus learning on the organisation's priorities and needs, as can an organisational learning day, which involves a wider group. Action learning projects provide a measurable and demonstrable focus for learning.

In brief

- It is important to develop a clear image of your present state. This can be helped by understanding how others see you, and a variety of questionnaires.
- The direction for the self-development process is often clarified by preparing a plan, whose format is less important than an individual's commitment to it.
- Continuing professional development is widely recognised as important – and it requires a plan, which can be formulated in a learning set.
- Get into the habit of compiling a learning log of rich events that happen to you – and do so – daily.
- Consider doing some biography work to deepen your sense of the movement of your life.

■ Use the U-process as a sampler for exploring biography work.

■ Use any of the recommended self-development texts as a way of generating an agenda for your development agreement and some ideas for action.

■ Learning is enhanced through support and challenge from one's peers.

■ A process for group meetings helps keep the focus on action *and* reflection.

■ Facilitators, though not essential, can help greatly in guiding the group's progress.

■ Self-development is nurtured by being linked to strategy and work-based action.

■ Half-way workshops are an opportunity to reconnect self-development with strategy, to recommit oneself, and to refocus.

■ Action learning projects provide a measurable and demonstrable focus for learning.

■ Final-day workshops serve to mark the end of the formal process and the start of continuous learning.

■ Organisational learning days provide a chance to learn from others' experience.

References

1   SENGE P. *The Fifth Discipline*. New York, Doubleday. (1993)

2   INGLIS S. *Making the Most of Action Learning*. Aldershot, Gower. (1994)

3   PEDLER M. and BOYDELL T. *Managing Yourself*. 2nd Edition, London, HarperCollins. (1995)

4   MEGGINSON D. and PEDLER M. *Self-development – A facilitator's guide*. Maidenhead, McGraw-Hill. (1992)

5   WHITAKER V. *Managing People*. London, HarperCollins. (1994)

6 ARGYRIS C. *Organizational Learning: A theory of action perspective*. Reading MA, Addison Wesley (1978)

7 CUNNINGHAM I. *The Wisdom of Strategic Learning. Maidenhead*. McGraw-Hill. (1994)

8 FRITCHIE R. 'Biography work: the missing part of career development'. *Industrial and Commercial Training*, Vol. 22, No. 2, pp 27–31. (1990)

9 HONEY P. 'Establishing a learning regime.' *Organisations and People*. Vol. 1, No. 1, pp 6–9. (1994)

10 McGILL I. and BEATTIE L. *Action Learning: A practitioner's guide*. London, Kogan Page. (1992)

Valuing Self-Development

Self-development can be of value to a whole range of stakeholders, namely to:

- individuals engaged in self-development
- the colleagues of self-developers
- the organisation in which the self-developers work
- the human resource (HR) department within the self-developers' organisation
- the facilitators of self-development programmes.

This chapter explores the benefits that each stakeholder can gain from their contact with self-development, and offers examples to stimulate your own explorations of the benefits of self-development.

The benefits to individuals

The benefits to an individual involved in self-development are highly varied. Each person creates a personal development plan (PDP) unique to them and their situation. Some people achieve their plans; others are in situations in which they change their plans in response to circumstances. In the latter situation people often find that the learning that comes from responding to the unexpected is greater than the learning that they would have gained from pursuing the original objectives they set themselves. Reflective individuals often plot their learning round the learning cycle: they do something, reflect on it, make sense of it, and then do things differently.

We know of many people who have been promoted or gained better jobs in different organisations during, or shortly after, self-development programmes. One chief executive said that the skills he learnt during his participation in a programme helped him to get the job that he had always wanted in another organisation. This may be seen as a major disadvantage for some organisations, because it increases staff turnover. However, self-development crystallises in many cases a dissatisfaction with the *status quo* that, if it had not been addressed, would have left the individual performing below what was required for the job.

By contrast, in some of our self-development programmes in the civil service, which involved short secondments to other organisations, participants returned with an enhanced appreciation of their own workplace, saying 'We're not as bad as we thought' or 'I always thought I wanted to work in the private sector, but now I'm not so sure.'

People can feel so energised from participating in a self-development programme that they approach their work in a different way: they try out new ideas or work more dynamically or flexibly, sometimes tackling old problems that were swept under the carpet years before.

Sometimes the benefits are not immediately obvious, however. Now and then, an individual leaves a self-development programme feeling confused and angry; he or she may have really struggled with letting go of traditional ways of work during the programme, and not seemed to have grasped the potential of working differently, despite everyone's best efforts to convince him or her. Yet, on occasions, we meet such people months or even years later only to find them singing the praises of self-development, having gradually resolved their problems. Others, sadly, who have chosen to put scant effort into a self-development programme reap equally scant benefits that transform neither themselves nor those around them.

When exploring the benefits experienced by a number of people attending a self-development programme, it is well to remember that their plans are highly individualised, and that the outcomes arising form each plan will therefore differ: one individual may address largely personal issues whereas another may want to focus on the strategy of the organisation, for example. Yet even if two or more people explore the same issues they may still choose to develop themselves in different ways. If four members of a learning set had given themselves as an objective to work on the impact that they made in meetings, for example,

∎ one could increase his impact by making more confident presentations

∎ another might decide to change her style because she recognised that her powerful presence was inhibiting others

∎ a third might work on increasing her influence on senior management

∎ the fourth might aim to enthuse his staff.

For this reason, evaluating the effect on individuals of self-development programmes should allow each person's changes to be expressed *in their own terms*. Questionnaires that homogenise people's replies lose the uniqueness of the outcomes of self-development. They are therefore to be avoided.

The Post-it process

The following is an approach for evaluating individual change that provides a full, accurate, and convincing set of outcomes:

1   Ask all individuals to write down in their own words what they have changed, putting each change on a separate Post-it.

2   Put these Post-its on a large board or a wall.

3   Group members then arrange these outcomes in clusters that hang together in some way significant to the members.

4   Members give a name to each of the clusters.

5   The evaluator takes these named groups and writes them up as a coherent and individual account, in the participants' own terms, of the changes.

Lewisham: individual outcomes

In the London Borough of Lewisham's successful bid for a National Training Award for its senior management self-managed learning programme the following claim was made for individual training benefits from the programme:

> Beyond the benefits of any specific skill or knowledge learning…there was also a very important development of the ability to learn, and manage their own learning…Other reported benefits have included:
>
> learning how to listen actively
>
> experiencing increased confidence
>
> recognising own skills/abilities
>
> understanding how to use other people as a resource
>
> realising the power and value of networking
>
> gaining the courage to face and manage change
>
> surviving and growing in an unstable climate
>
> recognising different perceptions/perspectives and valuing diversity
>
> regaining and clarifying personal power and control
>
> increasing effectiveness in managing people
>
> receiving and giving feedback on performance.

This is an example of the individual benefits presented to an official evaluation forum in a way that allows each person's change to be heard and valued.

The benefits to colleagues

When someone is being dynamic and seeking new ways of doing things, he or she can often involve others in the improvements: self-developers are encouraged to share part, or indeed all, of their PDP with their colleagues, if appropriate. Often colleagues or teams are keen to work with self-developers on the latters' issues, because such issues affect their own work too.

If a number of people within a team are on the same self-development programme they can challenge and support each other to do things differently.

The benefits to the organisation

The more self-developers there are within an organisation, the greater the increase in effectiveness is likely to be. ICL is currently evaluating the benefits gained from the participation of 1,200 of their staff in self-development programmes.

There are good economic reasons for evaluating any developmental programme, and some of the guidelines for doing so are relevant to self-development programmes. It is helpful to:

- evaluate the programme using an independent person or organisation
- evaluate against the objectives that were set at the beginning of the programme
- evaluate how the programme has influenced the way participants do their work.

Every self-development programme is uniquely tailored to the needs of the particular organisation, which evaluation should address. Some programmes focus on changing the culture or the way things get done; others on releasing more potential within the staff; yet others on implementing a new strategy or achieving business goals. These factors need to be included in the evaluation.

The parties involved in the programme can be brought together to explore its effect using the Post-it process for individual learners (see page 91). When we use this process for evaluation, attention centres on whether the programme had the desired outcome.

Lewisham: organisational outcomes

The Lewisham programme, whose individual benefits were outlined above, led, it was claimed, to the following organisational benefits, which again are taken from a fuller case made in their successful claim for a National Training Award:

> What the organisation was looking for...was a change...from a rigid, role-centred culture which operated on a command and control basis, to a more flexible, outcomes-oriented culture, in which managers utilised their own and others' resources and ideas to get things done... The qualitative difference in management style has been visible and continues to influence the way Lewisham now operates. For instance:
>
> ▮ Managers now network much more freely across the authority... This has considerably speeded up decision-making and action, and by encouraging cross-functional working it has eliminated much duplication and/or reinvention;
>
> ▮ Managers now understand how important daily, life-long learning is to personal and organisational survival;
>
> ▮ Some of the organisation's previous low-risk behaviour patterns...have been changed into support for new ideas and innovation through a better understanding of how people can learn from success and failure...managers are learning how to provide services differently or to provide more for less;
>
> ▮ An unexpected...benefit has been inter-cultural and gender learning resulting from the mixture of black and white managers and male and female managers on the programmes.

These were largely cultural outcomes, but they had bottom-line benefits as well.

Benefits from action learning projects

As we said in Chapter 4, one of the most direct ways of illustrating bottom-line benefits is to go the action learning route and encourage participants to carry out projects with tangible and measurable outcomes. One programme we were involved in for a transport company showed benefits 15 times the cost of the programme. The effect of another programme (in the steel industry) is illustrated by the fact that managers generated improvements worth over £1 million as a result of their projects.

The benefits to the HR department

Many HR co-ordinators have become so involved with self-development that they have arranged to participate in the programme themselves. One of the internal co-ordinators for the development programmes in the Employment Department chose to change the direction of his career as a result of his participation. He moved from administering training to a full-time involvement in designing and delivering development initiatives. Another co-ordinator used his language skills to set up a placement in Germany which led to an on-going exchange programme between that country and the UK.

John Stannard is a trainer at the Peak National Park who worked with us as a facilitator on three programmes for the Park. His background was in organising and delivering training courses, so the change of style to being a facilitator was initially quite a contrast. Working as facilitator within his own organisation meant that he had to address such issues as objectivity and confidentiality in encouraging the discussion of personal concerns among senior managers in the organisation.

We established our own facilitators' action learning set,

which met regularly, following participants' learning sets. During this time each of us shared our reflections on our participants' learning set and were challenged and supported by the other two facilitators as we analysed our progress. We then sought ways of setting ourselves demanding goals to achieve in the facilitation of our next learning set. The focus of our meetings was facilitator development, and the confidentiality of participants' issues was upheld throughout. We all learnt a great deal from these meetings, and enjoyed the rigour of working with our colleagues.

When we met John recently he described this participation as a facilitator as the most significant self-developmental experience he was involved in at that time. It changed both the way he viewed his work and his home life. He uses the enabling skills that he has developed to facilitate team development and problem-solving workshops for staff.

The benefits to the facilitators

We ourselves learn and grow during every programme we facilitate. At the design stage we get together with the facilitators and identify, and evaluate, each person's strengths so that we can plan the programme together to incorporate those strengths.

At the end of each stage of a programme we have a 'wash-up': we look back and assess what went well and what we plan to do differently. We often learn more from the things that have not gone so well, or did not work according to plan, rather than from those that occurred without a hitch.

We have talked to many of the facilitators who have worked with us and asked them about their learning. A striking example is provided by our colleague, Ian Flemming, and we describe this in the next section.

A facilitator's self-development over 10 years

Ian has worked as a facilitator on a number of action learning-based management development programmes. To explore his self-development over the last 10 years we asked him what he valued about this method of self-development and what he had learnt from our work together.

Figure 16, opposite, is a force-field analysis that highlights the factors that helped Ian's development and those that hindered it. It is interesting to note that Ian has many more helping than hindering factors. He has listed 'trauma' and 'loss' as *helping* factors because they shocked him into a reappraisal of his life and values. This proved to be highly developmental.

One of the principles of force-field analysis is that if you only increase helping forces, this will generate new hindering forces in an equal and opposite reaction. This reminds us that the most effective way of progressing towards your desired state is to reduce or eliminate the hindering factors. Some of Ian's hindering factors have already been eliminated. He ceased employment with the local authority in 1985 and is now a partner in a successful training consultancy. His other hindering factors are internal ones, which he has the power to influence. He has been consciously working on these and reducing their effect on his life over the last 10 years. In spite of maintaining, and indeed enhancing, the degree of balance in his life between home, work and leisure, Ian has also made space to start a new IT training and systems business (to provide stability and steady growth) using and extending his consultancy's existing skills.

Figure 16

FORCE-FIELD ANALYSIS: 10 YEARS OF SELF-DEVELOPMENT

BY IAN FLEMMING

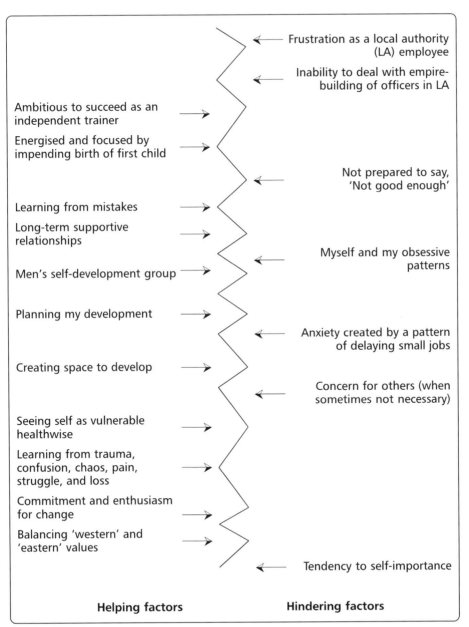

Helping factors | Hindering factors

Frustration as a local authority (LA) employee

Inability to deal with empire-building of officers in LA

Ambitious to succeed as an independent trainer

Energised and focused by impending birth of first child

Not prepared to say, 'Not good enough'

Learning from mistakes

Long-term supportive relationships

Myself and my obsessive patterns

Men's self-development group

Planning my development

Anxiety created by a pattern of delaying small jobs

Creating space to develop

Concern for others (when sometimes not necessary)

Seeing self as vulnerable healthwise

Learning from trauma, confusion, chaos, pain, struggle, and loss

Commitment and enthusiasm for change

Balancing 'western' and 'eastern' values

Tendency to self-importance

At the end of our interview we asked Ian to summarise the changes that had occurred as a result of his continuing commitment to self-development. He is now:

- capable and powerful
- passionate about learning
- very open-minded
- extremely committed to the work that he does
- a challenging and supportive mentor
- developing his career through using images of how he would like to be
- simplifying his life.

In brief

In this chapter we have suggested how you can evaluate the benefits of self-development for a whole range of stakeholders. In reviewing a process of self-development, consider the benefits to:

- individuals engaged in self-development
- the colleagues of self-developers
- the organisation in which self-developers work
- the HR department within the self-developers' organisation
- the facilitators of self-development programmes.

Tools and Resources for Self-Development

Introduction

Clearly the crucial 'tool' for self-development is ourselves, our own consciousness. Equally clearly, just relying on ourselves is not enough. Self-development works best as a social process – involves other people. The rest of this book is about how to make the most of ourselves and others in self-development. This chapter focuses on non-personal resources that we can employ alongside the help we derive from ourselves and others.

We shall explore the following resources, giving references for tracking them down and also some suggestions about how they might best be used:

- reference books
- workbooks
- instruments
- electronic networks
- organisations.

Reference books

Reference books offer a range of insights into how self-development can be pursued at a personal level and also in setting up schemes for others. There are books specifically about self-development, which we list first, but there is also a huge literature about related topics that we have dipped into, choosing classic books or recent texts which give you further sources in their indexes.

Self-development texts

BONES C.
The Self-reliant Manager. London, Routledge. (1994)
A business-oriented basic text by the organisation development manager of United Distillers.

BOYDELL T. and PEDLER M.
Management Self-development: Concepts and practices. 3rd edition, Farnborough, Gower. (1994)
Classic text laying out the concerns of the field. Makes the crucial distinction between development *by* self and development *of* self.

MEGGINSON D. and PEDLER M.
Self-development: A facilitator's guide. Maidenhead, McGraw-Hill. (1992)
Comprehensive text addressing self-development at individual, group, and organisational levels. Provides a framework for new facilitators or facilitators who are unfamiliar with the concept of self-development.

PARIKH J.
Managing Your Self. Oxford, Blackwell. (1991)
Attempts a synthesis of Western science and Eastern wisdom; a valuable book for those seeking balance in their lives.

PEDLER M., BURGOYNE J., BOYDELL T. and WELSHMAN G. (Eds).
Self-development in organisations. Maidenhead, McGraw-Hill. (1990)
A range of readings from practitioners in the field, offering current practices and challenges for the future.

Career development texts

CLARK F. A.
Total Career Management. Maidenhead, McGraw-Hill. (1992)
Offers thoughtful frameworks for both individuals and those planning the careers of others.

Individual development texts

CLUTTERBUCK D.
Everyone Needs a Mentor. 2nd edition, London, IPD. (1991)
The classic British text on mentoring, with practical advice and theoretical frameworks.

MEGGINSON D. and CLUTTERBUCK D.
Mentoring in Action. London, Kogan Page. (1995)
A development of *Everyone Needs a Mentor*, this book offers a range of organisational and individual cases, together with new frameworks for the practice of mentoring.

MUMFORD A.
How Managers Can Develop Managers. Aldershot, Gower. (1993)
Clear and practical advice on how to develop others in the context of work itself, grounded in the author's elegant conceptualisation of the learning process.

Group development texts

CUNNINGHAM I.
The Wisdom of Strategic Learning. Maidenhead, McGraw-Hill. (1995)
An interesting presentation of issues and approaches to putting development to work in organisations.

INGLIS S.
Making the Most of Action Learning. Aldershot, Gower. (1994)
A prescription for how to go about developing an action learning programme.

McGILL I. and BEATTY L.
Action Learning. London, Kogan Page. (1992)
Offers a range of approaches to action learning and outlines their uses.

PEDLER M. (ed.)
Action Learning in Practice. 2nd edition, Aldershot, Gower. (1991)
This book sets the scene and develops the areas of delight and concern in the practice of action learning.

Self improvement texts

ROBBINS A.
Awaken the Giant Within. London, Simon and Schuster. (1992)
This is written for those who find words like 'personal power' and 'destiny' attractive. Despite the rhetoric, there is sound advice grounded in a huge experience of developing and using the concepts he introduces.

New approaches to managing

MORGAN G.
Imaginization: The art of creative management. Newbury Park, CA, Sage. (1994)
Uses images and metaphor to help you transform the way you manage and work in organisations. An accessible and enjoyable book.

WHITAKER V.
Managing People. London, HarperCollins. (1994)
Introduces the concept of the manager as a provider of service to staff, who in turn provide a service to customers or clients. Has clear models and case-studies of managers who use these principles.

Re-engineering texts

ORAM M. and WELLINS R. S.
Re-engineering's Missing Ingredient: The human factor.
London, IPD. (1995)
Introduces the human factor into re-engineering, with five major case studies from organisations in the UK.

Large group interventions texts

JACBOS R. W.
Real-time Strategic Change. San Francisco, CA, Berrett-Koehler. (1994)
Offers a methodology for introducing change with large participative groups. Provides a how-to manual.

OWEN H.
Open-space Technology: A user's guide. Potomac, MD, Abbott. (1992)
Offers practice and theory of a method based on the participative gatherings that are the norm in many traditional societies.

WEISBORD M. *et al.*
Discovering Common Ground. San Francisco, CA, Berrett-Koehler. (1992)
A clear description of the methodology; also addresses the conceptual issues, allowing alternative perspectives their due, and is full of practical examples.

Organisational learning texts

CASEY D.
Managing Learning in Organisations. Buckingham, Open University Press. (1993)
Addresses self-managed and action learning groups before going on to explore organisational learning. Helpful models, grounded in experience of public and private sectors.

MAYO A. and LANK E.
The Power of Learning. London, IPD. (1994)
A comprehensive, grounded guide to practice, with much practical advice.

PEDLER M. and ASPINWALL K.
'Perfect plc'? Maidenhead, McGraw-Hill. (1996)
A questioning approach to the big issues of organisational learning that takes a moral perspective and addresses the particular concerns of the public sector in a separate chapter.

PEDLER M. BURGOYNE J. and BOYDELL T.
Towards the Learning Company. Maidenhead, McGraw-Hill. (1994)
Offers two key models and 101 glimpses of the path towards company learning.

SENGE P.
The Fifth Discipline. Doubleday, New York. (1993)
Offers a systemic approach to organisational learning that avoids simplistic assumptions and remains readable and practical.

Texts about learning

KOLB D.
Experiential Learning. New York, Prentice-Hall. (1985)
The classic text on learning from experience and learner-centred development. This book has a broad historical sweep, some well-validated research, models, and an inspiring vision of the learner at the centre of the learning enterprise.

MUMFORD A.
Effective Learning. IPD, London. (1995)
A wonderfully clear and concise summary of what learning is and how to bring it about in organisations by the man we rate as the UK's David Kolb.

Workbooks
Self-development workbooks/tapes

PEDLER M. and BOYDELL T.
Managing Yourself. 2nd edition, London, HarperCollins. (1994)
A small book for self-developers that packs a punch; many useful frameworks and activities.

PEDLER M, BURGOYNE J. and BOYDELL T.
A Manager's Guide to Self-development. 3rd edition, Maidenhead, McGraw-Hill. (1994)
Uses a model of 11 qualities of a successful manager to organise nearly 50 self-development activities, which also offer readings for further exploration.

COVEY S. R.
The Seven Habits of Highly Effective People. London, Simon and Schuster Audio. (1989)
A powerful presentation of Covey's basic ideas with enough detail to encourage immediate action; the tape is a useful stand-by for commuters.

Career development workbooks

BLOCH S. and BATES T.
Employability. London, Kogan Page. (1995)
A practical guide to considering one's own development; the focus is on business – individual rather than corporate.

FRANCIS D.
Managing Your Own Career. London, HarperCollins. (1985)
Offers a 12-step approach to career review and development.

Organisational learning workbooks

SENGE P. *et al.*
The Fifth Discipline Fieldbook. London, Nicholas Brealey. (1994)
Follows Senge's model of five disciplines, offering activities, examples, and sources for each.

PEARN KANDOLA.
Tools for a Learning Organisation. London, IPD. (1995)
A valuable set of tools and frameworks for enhancing organisational learning. Benefits from the best of the theory translated into practical applications and a style of presentation that is crisp and clear.

Instruments
Myers-Briggs Type Indicator

The questionnaire is restricted to those who have been trained to use it, but a large range of material concerning MBTI is available from:

Oxford Psychologists Press
Lambourne House
311–321 Banbury Road
Oxford
OX2 7JH
Tel.: 01865 510203
Fax: 01865 310368

Boydell and Pedler's Self-managing Climate Questionnaire

This short questionnaire is available in Pedler and Boydell's *Managing Yourself* referred to earlier in this chapter. Their Learning Company 11 Characteristics Questionnaire can be obtained from:

The Learning Company Project
28 Woodholm Road
Sheffield
S11 9HT
Tel. and fax: 0114 262 1832

Honey and Mumford's Learning Styles Questionnaire

The questionnaire, a booklet called *Using Your Learning Styles*, and *The Manual of Learning Opportunities* are all available from:

Peter Honey
10 Linden Avenue
Maidenhead
SL6 6HB
Tel.: 01628 33946
Fax: 01628 33262

Belbin's Team Role Inventory

The inventory and supporting material, including software that produces reports for teams based on how they need to develop given the mix of team roles preferred by team members, is available from:

Belbin Associates
Burleigh Business Centre
52 Burleigh Street
Cambridge
CB1 1DJ
Tel.: 01223 360895
Fax: 01223 365903

Margerison-McCann Team Management Development

These materials require the user to be licensed, having completed some training. Details can be obtained from:

Team Management Index
Team Management Development International
128 Holgate Road,
York
YO2 4DL
Tel.: 01904 641640
Fax: 01904 640076

The McBer Management Styles questionnaire

Details can be obtained from:

Hay Management Consultants
52 Grosvenor Gardens
London SW1 OAU
Tel.: 0171 881 7000

Electronic networks

There is an increasing proliferation of lists and networks that you can access through the Internet or the World-wide Web. The following items may therefore be of some interest to readers of this book.

MCB University Press provides a range of Internet conferences; you are advised to use World-wide Web to log on to INTERNET URL:http://www.mcb.co.uk

To subscribe to a management development list send a message to LISTSERV@MIAMIU.ACS.MUOHIO.EDU with no subject header and the following text in the body of the message: 'sub mgtdev-l *your name*'. Messages for the management development list go to: MGTDEV-L@MIAMIU.ACS.MUOHIO.EDU

To subscribe to the training and development list send a message to MAJORDOMO@MCB.CO.UK with no subject header and the following text in the body of the message: 'subscribe training-and-development'. Messages go to: TRAINING-AND-DEVELOPMENT@MCB.CO.UK

To subscribe to the learning organisation list send a message to MAJORDOMO@WORLD.STD.COM with no subject header and the following command in the body of your message: 'subscribe learning-org'. Messages go to: LEARNING-ORG@WORLD.STD.COM

Learning-org also has a home page and an archive on the Internet at: http://world.std.com/~lo.

Organisations

The two membership organisations in the UK with direct involvement in development are:

The Institute of Personnel and Development
IPD House
Camp Road
Wimbledon
London
SW19 4UX
Tel.: 0181 971 9000
Fax: 0181 263 3333

The Association for Management Education and Development
14–15 Belgrave Square
London
SW1X 8PS
Tel.: 0171 235 3505
Fax: 0171 235 3565.

In brief

This chapter has focused on non-personal resources that we can employ alongside the help we derive from ourselves and others. We explored resources, giving references for tracking them down, and also made some suggestions about how they might best be used.

Self-developers:

■ read books to develop insight into themselves and their work
■ explore workbooks and tapes to find new ways of working
■ use questionnaires to develop a truly realistic self-image.

8

Cultivating Self-Development

We all have the seeds of self-development within us. We need to create the right conditions to enable our seeds to grow. Self-development is not just for managers. All staff need to be engaged in lifelong learning if organisations are to thrive. Managers and HR professionals should therefore be like gardeners: it is their job to create the right conditions for the seeds of self-development to grow and blossom.

Sceptics say that some staff are too old or too dispirited to change. We disagree. Instead we work on the following assumption:

> Everyone has potential – in some people it is hidden and has to be identified by others.[1]

It is our job to help people to identify their seeds of potential development. There is an old saying:

> You can take a horse to water but you can't make it drink.

It is your task, as a manager or HR professional, to make your staff thirsty so that they will want to drink.

Creating the right climate for self-development

You can assist this process by creating the right conditions for growth. In this book we have described our experience and thoughts about self-development. We have also been encouraging you to experiment and do things differently. However, we are not necessarily suggesting that you do more.

In order to learn about self-development we have to do what may be new and different things: gain knowledge, reflect on our practice, resolve problems, and change the way we do things. Yet our purpose in doing this may be to do end up doing *less*, in a different way, so that we create time for high-quality reflection and 'professional idleness'.

Bertrand Russell talked about the concept of idleness in the 1930s.[2] He describes idleness in the following passage:

> When we talk about professional idleness we mean finding space for creativity – thinking – beyond the immediate, sharing insights, developing new ideas and new ways of working. Often we go outside of our work to do this and upset the balance of our lives by spending valuable leisure time focusing on work.

If we are to increase our creativity in order to do things differently at work, we may need to challenge traditional ways of working; this means identifying and implementing procedures that allow space for risk-taking and change. Ian Flemming (see Chapter 6) talks about creating 'risk vacuums': time set aside when new ideas can come in. Such time can also allow us to highlight other paradoxes inherent in self-development and to work with them.

The paradoxes of self-development

The Western approach to paradox is to try to resolve it. The Eastern view is to recognise that paradoxes exist in many issues and that we need to balance and work with the inherent contradictions. We have identified a number of paradoxes within the self-development process. We suggest that the Eastern approach is called for: of working with, rather than against, paradox.

Alone or with others

Self-development is about changing ourselves. Yet we cannot know accurately what to change unless we get feedback from others. It is also very useful to discuss feedback and plans for change with others to gain different perspectives on our own issues. By reporting on our progress to a group, some of us may well find that we are more likely to take risks and do things differently.

Ourselves alone?

Our development is about self and requires self-responsibility. Yet the process often works better with the help of the external facilitator of an action learning set, someone who does not get sucked into organisational politics or collude with the assumptions of the organisation. The facilitator can hold out the possibility of things being different and stand aloof from the pressures of the organisation, thus encouraging transformational change.

Focus on work and personal life

The career-planning that some people engage in as part of their self-development process can influence their whole lives. One participant chose to focus his immediate career-planning by going back and holding a 'conference' with his family to explore how they saw all saw themselves 10 years from then.

Change of self through action

Self-development has the potential to change both who we are and what we do. However, changes to self affect others only if we first change what we do and then gain feedback on this so that we can provide the service others are seeking.

Planned and emergent

When we are planning change we need a goal, so a PDP is of enormous value in getting us started. Yet as we work on our issues, new challenges and ideas emerge and may lead us to unexpected places where our learning is greater than originally planned.

A journey, not a destination

If we are to thrive in these fast-changing times then self-development needs to be a never-ending process. We cannot assume that what worked well in the past will work well again, because circumstances may well be different. Furthermore, we ourselves shall also have changed, because we shall have learnt from our experience. We need to be constantly re-evaluating our assumptions and behaviours to ensure that they are relevant to each new circumstance we encounter.

The first risks we take as part of our self-development process can seem demanding and difficult. Yet we find most people increasingly value and seek opportunities for risk-taking as they learn to enjoy the benefits of doing things differently. We encourage like-minded people to continue, after formal programmes are over, to work together informally or in self-development groups as fellow travellers on this journey of self-development. We like to remind them of the Latin phrase:

Nunc coepi – Now begin again.

References

1   Whitaker V. *Managing People*. London, HarperCollins. (1994)

2   Russell B. *In Praise of Idleness*. London, Unwin. (1991)

Index